PRINCIPLES
OF
TEACHING

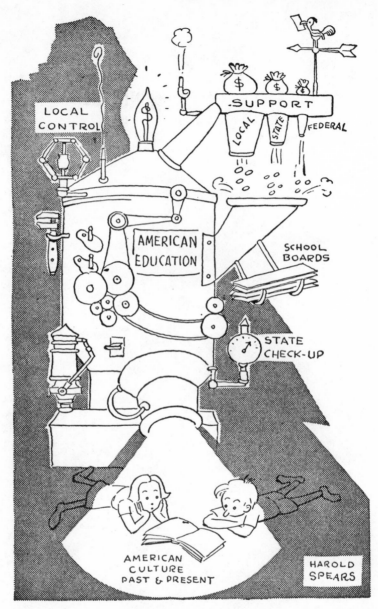

THE SOURCE OF LIGHT

PRINCIPLES OF TEACHING

ILLUSTRATIONS by the AUTHOR

Harold Spears

GREENWOOD PRESS, PUBLISHERS
WESTPORT, CONNECTICUT

Library of Congress Cataloging in Publication Data

Spears, Harold, 1902–
   Principles of teaching.

   Reprint of the ed. published by Prentice-Hall, New
York, in series: Prentice-Hall education series.
   1. Teaching. I. Title.
[LB1025.S679 1973]   371.1'02   72-106671
ISBN 0-8371-3374-2

PRENTICE-HALL EDUCATION SERIES

Editors

JOHN S. BRUBACHER

DAN H. COOPER

HAROLD SPEARS

Originally published in 1951 by
Prentice-Hall, Inc., New York

Reprinted with the permission of Harold Spears

Reprinted in 1973 by Greenwood Press,
a division of Williamhouse-Regency Inc.

Library of Congress Catalogue Card Number 72-106671

ISBN 0-8371-3374-2

Printed in the United States of America

To
DAVID

Preface to the Reprint Edition

THERE IS A TENDENCY IN SCHOOL PLANNING TODAY TO CONSIDER systems such as differentiated staffing, performance contracting, team teaching, and so on, which in themselves indicate the continued search for improved organization of the instructional day in the school. Commendable is this drive.

Regardless of overall structure, however, education at heart will always be a teacher working with a student, the interaction of the two comprising what school is all about. It is a human relationship that deserves continued attention.

H.S.

Preface

THIS BOOK IS THE RESULT OF REQUESTS FOR AN ENLARGE-
ment of the author's earlier book, *Some Principles of
Teaching*, which was received favorably by both elementary and secondary teachers, and apparently serves
as a handbook both on the campus and in the schools.

This enlarged version was requested by instructors for
use as a basic text for undergraduate courses dealing with
principles of teaching and for courses introductory to
teaching. It will serve both elementary and secondary
training courses. A large portion of the book is devoted
to the principles of classroom teaching. In addition to
this, it contains all the material originally included in
the smaller book and goes beyond that to treat the specific situation of the beginning teacher.

Among the topics fully developed are the teacher's market and the chances of employment, the student-teaching
assignment, the experiences faced the first year in an
actual teaching position, teacher welfare, and the teacher's
professional relationship with parents, laymen, administrators, pupils, and other teachers.

The author has attempted to treat in an understanding
way the situations that the typical beginner will face from
the student-teaching period on through the first year in

a regular teaching assignment, and to give the beginning teacher the benefit of his many years of experience.

It is not intended that this new book should replace the original, smaller edition. Rather, it is hoped that the small one will continue in use as a handbook of basic principles of teaching—for use by both beginning and experienced teachers, working at various levels of instruction.

H. S.

Contents

PART I

Teaching—*From the Position of the School*

PART I

Teaching—*From the Position of the School*

Chapter 1

The Study of Teaching

THIS IS THE STORY OF TEACHING. LIKE A NEWSPAPER STORY, it treats the *who*, the *what*, the *when*, the *where*, the *why*, and the *how* of the thing. Who teaches, and what? And when and where? Why do they teach, and how do they go about it?

1. *The modern American school is the result of human skill and enterprise rather than the product of hope and chance.*

To the early leaders of our nation goes the credit for realizing that the success of the American republic depended upon an extensive system of public schools, but it

remained for educators to implement that hope with the gradual elevation of teaching to a profession of careful preparation. From the day that a person enters a teacher training institution until the day that he teaches his last class, the job calls for careful study and preparation. It is not a magician's trade calling for tricks and sleight of hand. It is not a game or contest pitting child against teacher.

The study of teaching has three major points of emphasis or avenues of approach— (1) *the teacher,* (2) *the pupil,* and (3) *the school.* This is not to suggest any rank or order of importance in the study, but rather to suggest that all three are significant elements in any school situation. And each is the fountainhead of a long stream of courses in teaching offered at the graduate and undergraduate levels.

Table 1, on the next page, represents an attempt to trace teaching from each of these three approaches. The miscellaneous branches listed under each of the three suggest some of the various highly specialized courses that are taught in a graduate school of education. For instance, reading straight down column C, the School, these related courses are suggested:

    (1) the curriculum
    (2) educational sociology
    (3) child psychology and adolescent psychology
    (4) public school administration
    (5) state school systems
    (6) the teacher
    (7) administration and supervision
    (8) the history of education
    (9) extra-curricular activities
  (10) public relations.

TABLE 1

The ABC's of the Study of Teaching

A. The Teacher	B. The Pupil	C. The School
1. What he teaches (The curriculum)	1. What he learns (The curriculum)	1. What its program is (The curriculum)
2. How he teaches (Methods and techniques)	2. How he learns (The learning process)	2. What its purposes are (The cultural setting of the school)
3. Who he teaches (Nature of the pupil)	3. Who he is (Who goes to school)	3. Who attends it (Who goes to school)
4. Where he teaches (The field of teaching)	4. Where he goes to school (The field of teaching)	4. How it is organized (The organization of a school system)
5. With whom he teaches (Professional relationships)	5. How he is guided (Guidance program)	5. How it is controlled and supported (The legal provision for schools)

TABLE 1—*Continued*

A. The Teacher	B. The Pupil	C. The School
6. What conditions he teaches under (Teacher welfare)	6. Etc.	6. How it is taught (The teacher)
7. How he is supervised (School administration and supervision)		7. How it is administered (School administration and supervision)
8. Etc.		8. What its background is (The history of education)
		9. What is provided outside the classroom (Extra-curricular activities)
		10. How the public works with it (Public relations)
		11. Etc.

By reading down the other two columns of this same table, we can readily see some of the possibilities for separate courses that originate in the respective considerations of the teacher and the pupil. Also to be noted is the overlapping or close relationship of many of the items from one column to another. In undergraduate schools it is customary to sacrifice highly specialized or technical treatment of these miscellaneous branches of study and to offer, instead, introductory courses to teaching that treat the many relationships of the various parts of the job. That is the approach used in this book.

THE MECHANICS OF THE BOOK

There are three chief divisions of the book. The first part approaches teaching from the position of *the school,* the second from the position of *the pupil,* and the third from the position of *the teacher.*

Part I. Situated in the heart of the life of the community, the school holds a unique position in the American social scene. The hope and faith placed in it spring from the American way of doing things and are reflected in the broad expanse of the public school system over our land. This relationship of our schools to our society is developed in these chapters:

Chapter 2. Teaching Becomes a Profession
Chapter 3. The Place of the School in American
Life
Chapter 4. Governmental Responsibility for Education

Part II. The system of American education rests on principles and practices that have emerged from the study and experience of the profession. They represent the approach that good teachers take in their work—in their in and out of classroom relationships with their pupils. This relationship of the pupil and the teacher is treated in these four chapters:

Chapter 5. The Will and the Way to Learn

Chapter 6. The Teacher's Classroom

Chapter 7. The Pupil's Place in the School

Chapter 8. The Curriculum of the School

Part III. A teacher in training goes through a period of transition from student to teacher. To the study of the principles of teaching, such as those developed in Part II, is finally added the experience that comes through the student-teaching assignment. Then follows quickly the securing of a position and the break from the campus to an actual teaching position. No training program is actually complete without a short glance at the situations to be faced that first year on the job. This transition from student to teaching is considered in these six chapters:

Chapter 9. From Student to Teacher

Chapter 10. The Chances of Employment

Chapter 11. Succeeding on the First Job

Chapter 12. The Teacher and School Administration

Chapter 13. Professional Relationships

Chapter 14. The Teacher's Welfare

Basic Principles. In each chapter a number of basic principles treating the subject are emphasized. For the sake of the reader's convenience these are italicized and numbered consecutively throughout a chapter. Those in all fourteen chapters total 192. It might be said that these and the chapter titles form the framework on which the book is developed.

Topics for Discussion. The writer has placed a few discussion topics at the end of each chapter, with the intention of enabling the members of a class using the book to develop some thought provoking relationships between the material of the chapter and the conditions affecting teaching in their own state and locality.

Tables in the Book. The few tables used may give a first impression of austerity or one of over-detailed statistical treatment. The intention is to leave the reader with general appreciations rather than a storehouse of statistics that mean nothing in themselves. For instance, in Table 5, in Chapter 4, the general impression conveyed is that there is great variation among the states in the support of public education. The many facts are included only to convey this impression and to enable a reader to make some specific comparisons and draw some general conclusions about his own state.

A SCHOOL OF PRINCIPLES

Some years ago the school was looked upon as a mental filling station, quite removed from the give and take of community life. The school is no longer the ivory tower perched on a hill outside the town. It has long since put aside its medieval toga, put on its street clothes, and come down to mingle with the people. And in doing so, it has given the nod of recognition to the differences among children and among youth as they seek help in making their best adjustments and contributions to the commu-

THEN

nity life. Each year the school sees more clearly its unique function in American democracy.

2. *The American school has its being in the beliefs and aspirations of the American people and their way of life.*

Much of the credit for this goes to the research, experimentation, and deliberation that have come from the teaching profession itself. But much goes to the supporting society, the public who pays the bills, the fellow who asks for returns on his investment, returns that can be seen in the improved ways of people and communities.

The road down the hill, out of the clouds, leading into the affairs of boys and girls and men and women, has not been an easy one to find. There has been an attempt to emphasize in this book the principles that have stood out as beacons to teachers and administrators who have made the journey. May they act as guides to others who wish to make it. These principles that have weathered the test of classrooms all over America are taken not from the pages of books, but from the tongues and the actions of experienced teachers as they ply their trade day in and day out in the classrooms. These principles represent the working tools of the profession, but they are easier to recognize than to use. They are easier to endorse than to apply as practice.

There is a close relationship and at times an overlapping among the miscellaneous principles presented here. These similarities that appear call for no apology to the reader. The impossibility of drawing sharp distinctions need not

—AND NOW

be disconcerting to either author or reader, for teaching is to be looked upon as an interwoven human enterprise rather than as a manipulation of a collection of miscellaneous skills or techniques that can always be neatly classified.

In endorsing the recognition of individual differences, the author has humored himself by permitting some of the ideas to slip out in picture form rather than word form. Will the reader please consider the source to be the same? Although the book is organized to serve the would-be teacher in training, many of the principles may attract the attention of the experienced teacher in service. School methods will change with time and place; but educational principles, if they are psychologically sound and sociologically sincere, will serve indefinitely. The book is written for the beginning teacher, regardless of whether he is to teach in the elementary school, high school, or college. It is high time that we realize that the true principles of teaching recognize no artificial and manmade distinctions among grade levels.

WHO SHOULD TEACH

It is not the author's intention to say who should teach or who should not. However, by presenting as clearly as possible some of the realities of the job he may help indirectly some students of education who have not fully made their occupational decision. Throughout any treatment of teaching such as this, there are references to the qualities of a good teacher, some of which reflect innate characteristics and some of which reflect understanding that comes through either training or experience. Many teacher-training institutions include an interview as one of the means of determining which applicants for admission reveal the personal fitness and social alertness that promise success in the profession. For instance, the New Jersey State Teachers Colleges use the following rating blank in their interviews as an aid in the selection of students.[1]

INTERVIEW RATING SCALE

1. *General Appearance*—Those external qualities which characterize the individual.

0	1	2	3	4	5	6	7	8	9	10

POOR	AVERAGE	EXCELLENT
Is extremely unattractive. Moves awkwardly and is ungainly in posture. Lacks in personal grooming. Shows no discrimination concerning taste in dress.	Is fairly pleasing. Is dressed appropriately. Is clean and well groomed. Is coordinated in movements and has fair posture.	Commands attention. Is very well coordinated and has excellent carriage. Is faultlessly groomed and very well dressed.

[1] The rating scale is published here with the permission of Dr. Robert H. Morrison, Assistant Commissioner of Public Education in New Jersey, in charge of higher education, who was chairman of the committee that developed the scale.

2. *Voice*—The quality and volume of sound used in speech.

0	1	2	3	4	5	6	7	8	9	10

POOR	AVERAGE	EXCELLENT
Is monotonous, weak or harsh. Is unpleasantly pitched. Is lacking in resonance and clarity. Irritates the listener.	Is sufficient in volume and range. Is clear. Does not irritate the listener.	Is clear, free, pleasing, carrying and convincing.

3. *Use of Oral English*—The utilization of spoken English in communicating thought to others.

0	1	2	3	4	5	6	7	8	9	10

POOR	AVERAGE	EXCELLENT
Uses drab and commonplace words. Is inaccurate in sentence structure. Is confused and illogical in conversation. Has difficulty in conveying meaning.	Uses good simple English expressions with a reasonable degree of acccuracy. Is fairly well understood in conversation and in making simple explanations.	Uses a variety of words with precision and with faultless sentence structure. Is clear, colorful and convincing in discussion.

4. *Manner and Poise*—Deportment with respect to accepted rules of social conduct and bearing.

0	1	2	3	4	5	6	7	8	9	10

POOR   AVERAGE   EXCELLENT

Is crude, uncouth, unconvincing and weak. Bearing is a distinct handicap.

Extends the usual courtesies in meeting people. Generally impresses people favorably.

Is at ease, courteous, refined and gracious. Is convincing in impressing others favorably.

5. *Responsiveness During Interview*—Readiness and accuracy in response. Enthusiasm and quickness in understanding.

0	1	2	3	4	5	6	7	8	9	10

POOR   AVERAGE   EXCELLENT

Answers questions briefly. Shows no enthusiasm and makes inaccurate responses. Appears ill at ease or is unpleasantly conceited. Is very slow in grasping the most obvious.

Expresses interest and makes a fair attempt to carry on the conversational responses. Is at ease. Grasps the obvious quickly.

Shows an eagerness to respond. Is composed and self-confident without being unpleasantly conceited. Grasps new ideas quickly. Adjusts thinking to new situations readily.

INTERVIEW RATING SCALE—*Continued*

6. *Interest in the College Program*—Eagerness to learn about the courses of study and activity programs in college.

0	1	2	3	4	5	6	7	8	9	10

POOR   AVERAGE   EXCELLENT

POOR	AVERAGE	EXCELLENT
Asks no questions about the college. Does not respond when given an opportunity to ask questions. Expresses little curiosity about the college program.	Asks some questions about the college program. Shows interest in some phases of the college activities.	Shows enthusiastic interest and asks intelligent questions about the course of study, clubs, athletics, laboratories, equipment and student activities.

7. *Interest in People*—Concern for one's associates and their activities.

0	1	2	3	4	5	6	7	8	9	10

POOR   AVERAGE   EXCELLENT

POOR	AVERAGE	EXCELLENT
Has no interest in group activities. Seems self-centered and solitary.	Has participated with enjoyment in group activities. Seems to like people.	Is enthusiastic about other people. Has participated in a variety of group activities.

INTERVIEW RATING SCALE—*Continued*

8. *Interest and Taste in the Arts*—Awareness of and participation in the cultural aspects of living embodied in such fields as music, literature and painting.

0   1   2   3   4   5   6   7   8   9   10

POOR	AVERAGE	EXCELLENT
Reveals low standards or entire lack of interest. Is not aware of the arts as a field of culture.	Indicates some interest in at least one of the arts. Is intelligent in expressing likes and dislikes.	Shows diversity of interest and discriminating taste in two or more fields.

9. *Interest in Vocational Choice*—Concernment about choosing an occupation to which one will devote his life.

0   1   2   3   4   5   6   7   8   9   10

POOR	AVERAGE	EXCELLENT
Has no knowledge about different vocations. Shows no realization of the importance of choosing a vocation.	Is considering several vocations and believes he might enjoy any one of them. Has a fair knowledge about different vocations.	Has definitely chosen a vocation. Gives intelligent reasons for his choice. Has a keen insight into the vocation selected.

10. *Judicial Attitude*—Disposition to weigh and consider before formulating conclusions.

0	1	2	3	4	5	6	7	8	9	10

POOR	AVERAGE	EXCELLENT
Is likely to answer without giving thought to the question. Is notably lacking in balance and restraint.	Is aware that there are two sides to every question. Will probably make unbiased decisions under ordinary circumstances.	Is likely to weigh all factors pro and con in reaching decisions. Inspires confidence in ability to reach fair and sound conclusions.

For sometime yet, teaching is not going to get all the fine candidates that it needs. However, the ranks are full of fine teachers and the percentage will continue to increase decade by decade. Teaching has made great strides this century, thanks to such influences as the improvement of teacher training, the better selection of candidates for training, and the increased public support of the schools. Teaching is no longer a job—it is a profession. It ranks in importance with other high social callings such as medicine and dentistry, which also demand high character and an extended period of professional training.

Topics for Study and Discussion

1. What steps are taken at the local teacher-training institution to admit to the teacher-training course only those students who have the ability and personal characteristics suitable for teaching?

2. What provisions are made by the institution to direct into other lines of study those students who do not live up to these expectations?

3. Are there any fields of professional study on the campus that attract students of higher average ability and promise than those attracted to the field of teaching?

4. What provisions, if any, might be made for an improvement in the system of admitting candidates to the teacher-training course?

5. What are the more commendable features of the interview rating scale reproduced in this chapter?

6. Compare the local courses in teacher training with the areas of study included in Table 1.

THE COLONIAL
SCHOOLMASTER

THE TEACHER
TODAY

THE GROWTH OF THE PROFESSION

Chapter 2

Teaching Becomes a Profession

THE TEACHING PROFESSION HAS MADE GREAT STRIDES SINCE the early days when chief qualifications for a teaching position were the ability to mend quill pens and the strength to apply the rod. The menial beginnings of the profession are scattered through the diaries, letters, journals, and other records that have come down from early America.

In 1751, for instance, when the Public Academy of Philadelphia was opened, its trustees set down in black and white their noble purposes, stating first, that the new school was to train "a number of our Natives qualified to bear Magistracies, and execute other public offices of Trust, with Reputation to themselves and Country"; and second, that "a number of the poorer Sort will be hereby qualified to act as Schoolmasters."

Not until this century has teaching been able to shake itself loose from its poor relations, emerging onto the public scene as a profession of highest public trust calling for protection from "the poorer Sort," who might be elbowed into it by the more competent rushing to other callings. To the professionalization of teacher training goes much of the credit for the advancement.

Good schools of education today rank in prestige with good schools of medicine, law, or business. There has been a steady improvement in the science of teaching since the first teacher training institution was established in Concord, Vermont, in 1823 and the first normal school in Lexington, Massachusetts, in 1839.

1. *The quality of the teaching profession will continue in direct proportion to the quality of the professional training afforded the average teacher.*

Naturally, as long as teaching was a job calling for little if any special preparation, it could never have taken on the respect and stature that is now afforded it in the four- and five-year professional courses leading to certification. With the longer period of preparation came better standards of instruction as well as better working conditions for the teachers themselves. Adequate salaries, equitable salary schedules, provisions for sick leave and tenure, and similar improvements in working conditions reflect the overall upgrading of teaching in this century.

2. *In teaching today, the higher the level of salaries and the more advanced the teacher welfare provisions, the higher the standards of training, certification, and performance.*

Elsbree, who has given us one of the most scholarly studies of the history of *The American Teacher*, reaches this perplexing conclusion after carefully reviewing the early records:

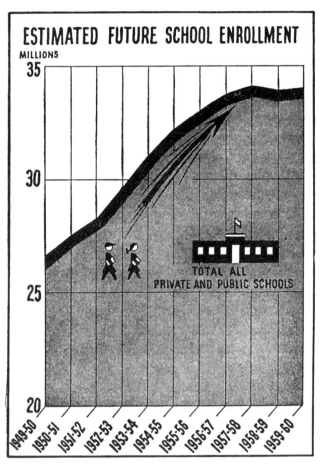

FIG. 1. ESTIMATED SCHOOL ENROLLMENT IN THE NATION,
1950 TO 1960.[2]

2 Figures 1 and 2 were prepared by the Research Division, National
Education Association, and appeared first in *Our School Population*,
Reproduced with permission of that Office.

The colonial schoolmaster is unclassifiable. He was a God-fearing clergyman, he was an unmitigated rogue; he was amply paid, he was accorded a bare pittance; he made teaching a life career, he used it merely as a steppingstone; he was a classical scholar, he was all but illiterate; he was licensed by bishop or colonial governor, he was certified only by his own pretensions; he was a cultured gentleman, he was a crude-mannered yokel; he ranked with the cream of society, he was regarded as a menial. In short, he was neither a type nor a personality, but a statistical distribution represented by a skewed curve.[1]

Still a noticeable fraction of the public place themselves on the teacher's level in the ability to tell how the job should be done in the classroom—a liberty the layman would not take with the physician's position in the operating room. In spite of this fact, the advancement made this century in school standards, including teacher training and certification as well as financial support and administrative competence, has definitely boosted teaching to true professional status beside medicine, dentistry, engineering, and law. The day has passed when the case for training was easily dismissed with the statement that "good teachers are born." Certainly, good teachers are born, just as anybody else is born, but—

3. *Good teachers are not born good teachers; they achieve the honored position through proper preparation and experience.*

---

1 Willard S. Elsbree, *The American Teacher*, New York: American Book Company, 1939.

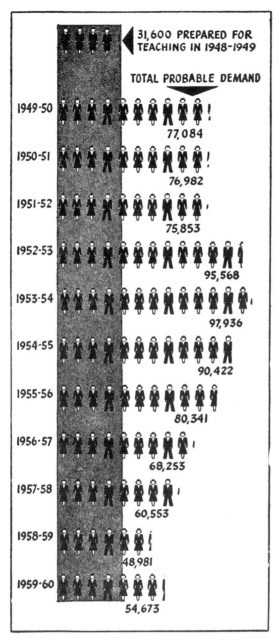

31,600 PREPARED FOR
TEACHING IN 1948-1949

TOTAL PROBABLE DEMAND

1949-50   77,084

1950-51   76,982

1951-52   75,853

1952-53   95,568

1953-54   97,936

1954-55   90,422

1955-56   80,341

1956-57   68,253

1957-58   60,553

1958-59   48,981

1959-60   54,673

FIG. 2. ELEMENTARY SCHOOL TEACHERS NEEDED, 1950 TO 1960,
COMPARED TO THE NUMBER NORMALLY TRAINED EACH YEAR.[2]

THE CHALLENGE AHEAD

Barring unforeseen events, teaching will face its greatest opportunity during the next ten or fifteen years. Or, on the contrary, by muffing the challenge to move into this period with proper foresight and preparation, it faces the possibility of having to sell its professional birthright for a mess of substandard pottage.

Simple Arithmetic. Insight into this situation asks for little more than an application of simple arithmetic. Figures 1 and 2, prepared by the research division of the National Education Association of the United States, indicate the possible opportunity—or the disaster—of this period that we are now well into. Behind the figures are such rapid calculations as these:

1. The schools need approximately 750,000 new elementary teachers between 1950 and 1960, to care for new classes and to replace teachers departing from service. The normal turnover of teachers as a result of death, resignation, and other causes is 7 per cent.

2. When this decade began, only about 30,000 elementary teachers were being trained annually.

3. When the period began, as many as 75,000 elementary classrooms were being handled by teachers with emergency or substandard licenses.

4. The great increase in elementary-school attendance, indicated in Figure 2, will reach the secondary school by 1956, and the demands for high-school teachers should increase 50 per cent over the demands of ten years ago.

To emphasize the bare facts of supply and demand in the teacher market is not to sound a pessimistic note about the period ahead. Rather it is to emphasize the stirring challenge that our profession faces as it moves more and more into a role of public significance and confidence. The chapters of this book emphasize preparation for that role.

WHERE DO WE TEACH?

4. *Where there are pupils, so there are teachers.*

The old maxim—where there is smoke, there is fire—suggests in this business of schooling that where there are pupils, so there are teachers. One who passes by this statement hastily as too simple for consideration, needs to be reminded that every year there are beginning teachers unable to secure positions because they have trained themselves in subjects for which there are not enough pupils, and at the same time there is a shortage of teachers in other areas.

This reflects in part the failure of the trainee to study the teacher market with an eye to pupil enrollment by

SUPPLY   AND   DEMAND

THE TEACHER AND HIS MARKET

grade or school level and by subject popularity. Likewise, a consideration of the supply of teachers is most helpful. Time and place have a lot to do with teacher markets.

The Time. For instance, in 1900 half of the pupils in high schools, both public and private, studied Latin. In 1935, in most high schools Latin was out, and there were 50 per cent more pupils taking French than Spanish. After 1940, French became a poor second to Spanish. It would be highly impractical for one to train for the foreign language field merely by personal like or dislike of a language.

The annual birthrates hold the key to total school enrollment by grades. The facts of present school enrollments and noticeable population trends are always in the records, available for any student of education who wishes to be very scientific in preparing for his field. We are indeed fortunate to have at our professional service at all times, two excellent research offices, that of the United States Office of Education and that of the National Education Association of the United States, both in Washington, D. C.

Shortages and excesses in teacher supply should seldom come as a statistical surprise. The high-school enrollment dropped after World War II, and a simple projection of lower-grade enrollments and birth rates indicated no great growth could be expected at the four-year high-school level until about 1956.

The shortage of elementary-school teachers in recent years reflected the entrance into the elementary schools in 1948 of the first detachment of the bumper crop of

wartime babies. The upward trend of the birth rate statistics indicated that by 1958 the elementary-school enrollment in America would have increased in fifteen years by
about 50 per cent. Barring a national emergency such
as war, the high-school cannot fail to have a boom between
1956 and 1960.

The Place. The trainee can fit into this picture of the
national teacher situation the unique conditions operating
in his own state or locality, and will come out with a fair
estimate of the teacher market and his possible place in it.
The fact that the population of the West Coast states at
the last census showed nearly a 50 per cent increase in a
decade, was accounted for by migration of population as
well as by higher birth rates. At the same time, a decline
in population in other areas of the nation was just as significant to teachers in training there.

State graduation requirements are also helpful in esti-
mating teacher needs, especially in the high-school field.
If the state of Indiana requires one year of mathematics
for graduation and a neighboring state requires none,
this tells something about possible mathematics jobs in
the two. If one state requires two years of American history and civics for graduation and another requires only
one, this is equally significant. If one requires two or
three times as much physical education as another, this
too is meaningful to those in training.

If a high school is in a well-to-do suburban community
where 70 per cent of the graduates go to college, there will
certainly be more foreign language and mathematics
positions in the school than in another of equal size located

in a large-city industrial neighborhood, where only 10 per cent of the graduates go to college.

Although there has been a shortage of well trained kindergarten teachers in the nation as a whole, the absence of kindergarten education in many sections of the country invites study and decision by one contemplating training for the field.

The Teaching Field. Many times the teacher market has been glutted with teachers with one type of preparation and short of teachers of another type. When there is a national overabundance of high-school teachers, usually the excess shows up first in the English and social studies— in spite of the fact that in any high school there are more positions in these instructional areas than in any other two. The oversupply of teachers in the two fields is a result of the great number of such courses required of all students in the typical teacher-training institution; it is relatively easy for the trainee to round out a major or a minor in the work and thus qualify for certification.

In 1948 and 1949 the high-school market was suddenly overstocked with social studies and boys' physical education teachers. By chance, or by common interest, a great percentage of the men who returned from war service and went back to college to pick up their teacher training, chose either one or both of these fields. Completing their training about the same time, they represented a teacher supply two or three times too great for the openings available. Finding a shortage of elementary teachers when seeking positions, many then returned to the campus to invest more time in qualifying for such certification.

5. *Regardless of the nature of the supply and demand in the teacher market, there is always a job for the well-prepared and promising teacher.*

When there is a shortage in the high-school field, it is usually in industrial arts, home economics, commerce, science, art, and music, in about that order. However, this general situation is tempered by time and place, and there are exceptions in many states or sections of states.

Four times out of five, and in four school districts out of five, for some time now it has been easier to secure an elementary-school position than a high-school position. There is nothing strange about this situation. It is mathematical, and there are a number of forces that create it.

1. In half of the school systems of America there are eight or nine grades in the elementary school and only four in the high school.

2. Practically 100 per cent of the children who begin school remain through the eighth grade, but only half of those who enter ninth grade remain to graduate from high-school.

3. The bumper crop of wartime babies presented the elementary school first with a phenomenal growth in number of classes—a growth that could not touch the high school until eight years later.

Furthermore, a teacher who prepares for the elementary school is certified for the whole field, for all the elementary grades. In getting a job, he has a great advantage over the high-school trainee who by certification rules in most states must gamble on training in a couple of subjects. The college official who guides trainees into their respective college courses, does not have to be a skilled bookmaker to point out to them these odds of employment.

As the schools of America turn the corner at the mid-century, the percentage distribution of teachers among the school levels would indicate that the trainee has twice as many openings ahead in elementary schools as in secondary, there being approximately two-thirds of a million teachers at the elementary level and one-third of a million at the other. As to the distribution of teachers by sex, the

BIG SCHOOL OR LITTLE SCHOOL?

ratio of women to men at the secondary level was somewhere between two-to-one and five-to-three, but at the elementary level there were a dozen women to every man.

The Size of Schools. Although the lack of space limits a full treatment of the subject here, for the teacher in training there is an interesting story about the various sizes of the schools in each state in which he may teach. It is usually surprising to the trainee who grows up in a city to discover the great number of small schools that exist. The typical American school, at either elementary or secondary level, is an extremely small school.

TABLE 2

Distribution of Students by School Level, United States [3]

School Level	Enrollment
Elementary Schools	
Public	20,674,000
Private and Parochial	2,887,000
Residential schools for exceptional children	60,000
Model and practice schools in teacher training institutions	37,000
Federal schools for Indians	28,000
Total elementary	23,686,000
Secondary Schools	
Public	5,452,000
Private and Parochial	635,000
Residential schools for exceptional children	10,000
Model and practice schools in teacher training institutions and preparatory department of colleges	40,000
Federal schools for Indians	5,000
Total secondary	6,142,000
Higher Education	
Universities, colleges, professional schools, including junior colleges and normal schools	2,700,000

[3] This was the estimate of enrollments for the school year 1950-51, as released by the United States Office of Education, September 5, 1950.

TABLE 2—*Continued*

School Level	Enrollment
Other Schools	
Private commercial schools	300,000
Nurse training schools (not affiliated with colleges and universities)	75,000
Total other schools	375,000
Grand Total	32,903,000

TABLE 3

Public High Schools by Size, United States [4]

Enrollment	Number	Per Cent	Enrollment	Number	Per Cent
1-9	234	1.0	300-399	1,467	6.0
10-24	975	4.0	400-499	919	3.8
25-49	2,689	11.1	500-749	1,458	6.0
50-74	3,119	12.8	750-999	793	3.3
75-99	2,548	10.5	1,000-1,499	808	3.3
100-149	3,657	15.0	1,500-2,499	561	2.3
150-199	2,266	9.3	2,500-4,999	150	.6
200-299	2,651	10.9	5,000 & Over	19	.1

[4] United States Office of Education statistics, the most recent at the time of publication.

Fully 75 per cent of the high schools have less than 300 pupils, and over half of them enroll fewer than 150 pupils. (See Table 3.) Although there has been a concerted effort toward the consolidation of small schools, of educational necessity there will continue to exist thousands of small high schools in the nation. The sparsity of population, as well as geographic conditions, makes this necessary. Severe weather in certain sections and shortages in roads likewise make it essential that small schools be continued in order to equalize educational opportunities. The experience that comes to a young teacher in a small high school can be broad and most valuable. Some of the most satisfying contributions are being made in these schools.

As to the elementary school, the range in size is tremendous, with the great mass being exceedingly small schools. Limited space requires us to omit the total breakdown and to review only the one-teacher schools.

THE ONE-TEACHER SCHOOL

"I began teaching in a one-room rural school."

Invariably this statement is made with great pride by those leaders of the teaching profession who have had that early experience. In fact, they are more apt to refer to it than to any other single assignment in their progress in the profession. College presidents and school superintendents of larger cities who began in a one-room school never hide that fact.

The one-teacher school, in disrepute for years because of its limited facilities and program, stands in the history of American education as the growing nation's frontier outpost against ignorance and inequality. It brought learning to children in the rural sections of the states and out-of-the-way sections of the country when they otherwise would have been denied such opportunities.

Interestingly enough, the one-teacher school still holds a significant spot in America's educational system and invites teachers trained specifically for the unique job. There are still 75,000 one-teacher schools, indicating that just about one out of every ten of America's elementary classroom teachers gives her service in these single-room schools.[5] Of the total of 171,500 public schools—146,000 elementary and 25,500 secondary—fully 44 per cent are one-teacher schools.

Their Location. Naturally most of these small schools are in the rural states. (See Table 4.) However, a few are found in even the larger cities of the country. For instance, San Francisco maintains a one-room, all-grade elementary school of approximately 15 children on Yerba Buena Island. The table reveals that: (1) in a third of the states, as many as half of the schools of the state are one-teacher schools; (2) in six states one-third to one-half are one-teacher schools; (3) in nine states one-fourth to one-third are such; and (4) in four states one-fifth to one-fourth are such.

Highly significant is the fact that in a state as large and as populous as Illinois, 75 per cent of the public schools are one-room schools, and in California and New York as many as one out of five are one-room schools. On the other hand, in the past thirty years a number of states have moved rapidly toward consolidated school districts,

---

5 The statistics used in this section were taken from the United States Office of Education study, Walter H. Gaumitz and David T. Blose, *The One-Teacher School—Its Midcentury Status*, Circular 318, 1950.

toward replacing small units with the centrally located school into which children are fed from all directions by a network of bus lines. For instance, today Ohio has only 5 per cent as many one-room schools as it had thirty years ago, Indiana only 7.6 per cent, Washington only 8.8 per cent, and Maryland only 9.8 per cent.

The number of one-room schools in the various states indicates the number of teachers employed in such schools. Almost half of the teachers of South Dakota teach in this type of school, 42 per cent in North Dakota, 37 per cent in Nebraska, 23 per cent in Minnesota, 27 per cent in Iowa, and 22 per cent in Missouri, Wisconsin, and Kansas.

The training institutions in the states in which this type of school is found in noticeable numbers are becoming more and more appreciative of the unique services offered by the teacher of such a school and are accordingly including appropriate training. The absence of an administrative officer in the school places upon the teacher added responsibilities in dealing with the school patrons and with the board of education.

PROGRESS IN EDUCATION

In another quarter of a century, the one-room school will have disappeared from most of the sections of the country, giving way to the efficiency that modern school administration has been bringing to taxpayers for some time and will continue to bring in larger and larger quantities. But wherever the school remains, loyal teachers will take their posts there to give service to the nation and to the individual child. Any beginning teacher who plans for the profession rather than for a job, who antici-

TABLE 4

One-Teacher Schools in the United States [6]

The States	Number of One-teacher Schools	Percentage of All Schools in the State
South Dakota	3,202	86.1%
Nebraska	4,434	79.3
Illinois	7,126	74.6
North Dakota	2,677	72.2
Wisconsin	4,475	70.6
Iowa	5,631	70.5
Minnesota	4,418	70.5
Missouri	5,125	67.0
Kansas	3,090	64.3
Wyoming	385	58.6
Montana	915	58.5
Georgia	1,758	58.4
Vermont	571	57.3
West Virginia	2,528	55.9
Kentucky	3,462	55.5
Michigan	2,952	53.3
Maine	728	39.2
Arkansas	1,450	39.0
Oklahoma	1,324	38.9
Tennessee	2,095	38.8
Nevada	88	37.3
Mississippi	1,850	36.2
Pennsylvania	2,744	32.8
New Mexico	263	32.2

TABLE 4—*Continued*

The States	Number of One-teacher Schools	Percentage of All Schools in the State
Virginia	1,078	29.1%
Idaho	270	28.2
Oregon	399	27.5
Louisiana	778	27.4
Colorado	561	27.3
South Carolina	1,019	26.2
Alabama	1,088	25.7
New Hampshire	133	21.5
New York	1,494	20.8
Delaware	48	20.3
California	820	20.1
Florida	420	17.7
Arizona	87	17.7
Texas	1,200	14.9
Maryland	165	14.1
Connecticut	115	13.1
North Carolina	595	12.7
Indiana	411	12.4
Ohio	446	10.2
Washington	155	9.9
Rhode Island	25	6.5
Massachusetts	128	5.6
Utah	28	5.5
New Jersey	89	4.9

6 United States Office of Education, Walter H. Gaumitz and David T. Blose, *The One-Teacher School—Its Midcentury Status*, Circular 318, 1950.

pates a long career rather than a trial period in teaching, should appreciate the opportunity available in the small schools—opportunity to grow and opportunity to serve. Teaching is an important undertaking, as important in the large city classroom as in the one-room school, in the large high school and the small.

The progress that schools have made during the past hundred and fifty years in America promises to continue. Just as the best days of instruction and educational opportunity are ahead, so are the best years of the teaching profession. Public support of and faith in the schools is highly dependent upon loyal, well prepared teachers who place child welfare first.

6. *The potential advancement of teaching is more dependent upon the efforts of those within the profession than upon the attitudes of the public.*

Good teachers mean good schools, and good schools bring public confidence and, in turn, adequate public support. The greater the percentage of inadequately staffed classrooms in a school system, the greater the percentage of disbelieving laymen and the greater the deficiencies in the school budget. As will be discussed at length in later chapters, the profession will advance just as long and as far as teachers do.

The teacher must first appreciate the true purposes of the school program, and feel those purposes rather than just recite them. He must understand sufficiently the basis of school organization in America, which involves the support and control of education by the people. These matters are reviewed in Chapters 3 and 4.

TOPICS FOR STUDY AND DISCUSSION

1. Are there any traces today of the public attitude toward teaching that was revealed by the trustees of the Public Academy of Philadelphia in 1751?

2. Secure from the proper office of the local college the numerical distribution of the students of education among the various fields of teaching: elementary education; secondary-school social studies; English; etc. Compare the distribution with the potential market for teachers in this state and draw conclusions.

3. From the two Washington, D. C., research offices mentioned in the chapter, secure the latest bulletins treating the market for teachers in the country as a whole, and make comparisons with the situation in this vicinity.

4. What guidance provisions are set up on the local campus to help the student of education choose a field of teaching that promises adequate openings?

5. In this state what has been the tendency in the consolidation of small school districts? This is the type of topic that could be very well discussed by a representative from the State Department of Public Instruction.

6. From the State Department secure data about the distribution of schools in the state by size and grade levels included, and prepare in chart form for group study and discussion.

Chapter 3

The Place of the School In American Life

1. *No teacher can expect to take to the first job an appreciation of the full significance of teaching.*

To a beginning teacher, the classroom full of children at hand seems to call for about all of his professional attention, and rightly so. But as time goes on and the breadth of the profession more fully reveals itself to the teacher, the classroom emerges in his understanding as a small but highly significant segment of the whole school, the whole community, and the whole American scene. It is then that he begins to show a sincere interest in seeking the answers to questions such as these:

1. What are the true purposes of the school?
2. Who assumes responsibility for the support and the control of the school? What are the unique functions of the local community, the state, and the nation in these matters?
3. What does the public actually expect of the school?

Although the provision for any detailed study of such questions as these is a function of the graduate school rather than the undergraduate school, it is well for the beginning teacher to take a peek at these things to come. For he needs to know early,

(1) that he doesn't have the freedom to set all of the purposes of his teaching, but that part of this job has been done by American society long before he enters the profession;

(2) that any state in the Union shares in great part the responsibility of education with the local community and in lesser part the responsibility with the Federal government; and

(3) that the public has great faith in what schools can do for children and youth, and reveals this faith in varied ways.

The teacher doesn't work alone. He is tied to the teacher in the next classroom and to the one across the country just as surely as he works side by side with the parent, the taxpayer, the school trustee, the superintendent, and the legislator. The increase in teachers' salaries in a neighboring community is most likely to be reflected in time in the local attitude toward salaries. The level of salaries in a large city in one part of a state bears influence upon those in a city of similar size in another part of the state.

The attack that is made upon the schools in the next county may spread in time to the local county. Likewise, the strength of a school program in a neighboring city may lend strength to the public feeling about schools in the local community. The weakness of the classroom next door makes the job more difficult for a teacher, just as strength next door means support.

THE SCHOOL'S PURPOSES

2. *The number-one purpose of the American school is to train for American citizenship.*

It is one thing to endorse preparation for American citizenship as the first task of the school; it is another to dissect American democracy into its specific principles and ideals; and it is yet another to set up a training program attuned to these principles and to the prevailing conception of how learning takes place.

Understanding will come from the school's program only if there is provided practice in, as well as knowledge of, the democratic way of life. Mere oratory, flag saluting, and anthem singing are not enough. They play an important place in the school, but these practices should grow out of and along with fundamental appreciations and teachings of democracy rather than be substituted for them. Freedom in democracy springs from civic responsibility, whether the action-situation be in the school society or in the larger society outside the school.

Self-direction in the school society, differentiated curricula, respect for personal differences in the classroom, individual instead of group standards of accomplishment, the selection of leaders from one's group to help handle room and all-school government, pupil-teacher planning of school work to be carried out by a class group, lessons in sportsmanship on the playing field and in courtesy about the building, practice in thinking critically through questions meaningful to those doing the thinking, pooling opinions with the group in co-operative attack upon a common problem, respecting the right of the other fellow to his opinion, and a hundred and one other practices that reflect the American way of life—these wherever used throughout the nation are conditioning school children and youth with a love of country that cannot be easily shaken.

An appreciation of American democracy must be taught; it cannot be left to chance. From knowledge taught and practice provided emerges such appreciation.

3. *The wholesome development of the pupil cannot be considered aside from the school's obligation to train for American democracy.*

The number-one purpose of the American public school is to train for American democracy, and the closely related number-two purpose is the education of each boy and girl, in so far as possible, to the limit of his capabilities. Although this interest in the welfare of the individual pupil reflects in itself the democratic appreciation of personal worth, it does not follow that this emphasis alone will assure the fulfillment of the number-one purpose of public education.

In fact, it is doubtful if the average layman truly appreciates this first obligation of the school. Parenthood in its very nature is child-centered and invites the parent to look upon the school chiefly as the means of improving the personal status of his own child in the world. His test of the effectiveness of the training given is more apt to be of the form that his child uses in written expression than of the social function to which he puts such knowledge. His test is more apt to be of his son's ability to make the team than of the cooperative tendencies he develops after

THE AMERICAN SCHOOL—THE SUPPORT OF THE INDIVIDUAL
CHILD AND THE AMERICAN WAY OF LIFE

so doing. His test is more apt to be of the marks made in the American history course than of any social consciousness of community affairs displayed by the son or daughter after having taken the course. And he is more apt to base his judgment of the secondary school on the success his son makes in college than on the percentage of all youth of high-school age that the school is able to hold until graduation. The true social purposes of education in American democracy are hazily, if at all, appreciated by the average taxpayer.

Which is to say that after all teaching has become a profession that marks the one properly trained in the work as more keenly aware of the function and the possible form of the educational program than the layman. The proven methods of teaching are to be learned in the institution that trains for the profession and are to be set in the experience that follows.

Teachers must attain this professional stature that comes with a thorough and unbiased study of their trade, and, once attained, this stature must be reflected in the improved lay understanding of the true purposes and maximum possibilities of organized schooling.

Parents as well as teachers must come to appreciate that the true effectiveness of a school is to be determined not by studying the marks of its graduates but by studying the graduates themselves and what they do. One might actually say that the ultimate test of today's school is tomorrow's community. And as the school moves ahead, it will at all times consider the wholesome development of the pupil and, at the same time, its obligation to train youth for American democracy.

4. *Classrooms and schools should represent a fine balance between cooperative endeavor and individual enterprise.*

There is something about the realities of life, and perhaps there always will be, that invites the school to lead each child to work for his good and to judge realistically what he can and cannot do. It is a noble thing for homo sapiens to stand on his own feet, rather than to depend upon his fellow creatures for his maintenance. It is likewise noble for him to achieve better things and to be able to move ahead on his own abilities and skills.

This individual enterprise might be called the more selfish side of the educational endeavor. Balancing it needs to be the classroom study of how our country has grown by means of the mutual respect and cooperative endeavor among her citizens. Balancing it also needs to be the cooperative endeavor of the pupils, endeavor that finds its goal in the common good rather than in the advancement of the individual for his own sake. Teachers must work at both tasks, and in doing so there is no reason for conflict between the two goals. They are the warp and the woof of the pattern known as the American way of life.

Since democracy can be maintained only if the people love their country and respect its laws, it follows that personal interest has to give way to public interest in the life of the citizen. In seeing that the personal interest of each child is served to a maximum in the school program, the teacher is not denied the opportunity to serve the group interest and the opportunity to strengthen in the child his knowledge of this basic principle of the American way of life.

Only through the protection of the common welfare can the individual advance in American life, and only through the advancement of the individual can the common welfare be protected.

5. *The business of the school is to make successes rather than failures.*

A school staff should never set itself up as a screening body to select among the children that come through its

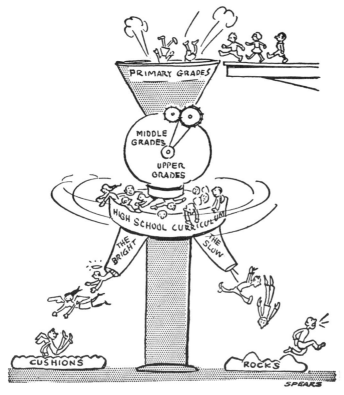

ANTIQUATED MACHINERY

classes, marking these as hopeful, these as questionable, and these as of no promise at all. The teaching function is to help children rather than to judge them, to take each as he comes and help him along as best we can.

There is always the teacher who hesitates to pass on to the next grade certain children who will be considered as unprepared by the teacher at that next level. There is always the teacher who fails a good percentage of the students who take his course, justifying in his own mind such failure on the basis of so-called standards. Retardation has its rightful place in school operation, but there is always the teacher who finds it easier to fail a child than to instruct him. There is always the teacher who fails a student as punishment for teacher assignments not carried out.

Failures in the first and second grade usually represent school expectations set beyond child maturity. At any grade level or in any subject field the school is challenged to discover the talents of the child, regardless of how dim they may be, and to capitalize and build upon them. To emphasize his weaknesses by penalizing him for them represents a process as financially wasteful to the public as it is psychologically unfair to the child.

The Nature of Schooling

6. *The good school does not limit its efforts to preparation for life, for it is life itself.*

If we conceive schooling as mainly picking up this course, this skill, and this fact for possible future use, it would naturally follow that in this race for the promised land ahead—adulthood—children and youth should skip

grades and cut corners as they cleverly beat out their com-
petitors. But if we don't guard against it, this fallacious
thinking will saddle us with a school promising no immediate satisfaction to the student, a cold-blooded school
that tips its hat not to children but only to honors, awards,
credits, marks, promotions, and graduation—yes, a graduation presented as the acme of it all, a commencement
bolstered with its "thank-goodness-that's-past" attitude.

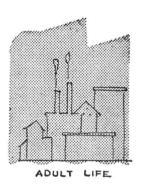

ADULT LIFE

WHAT'S THE HURRY, LAD?

In our intense interest to hurry young people on to
something ahead in life, rather than to help them to live
richly and fully at all age and grade levels, we will be
granting the AB degree at the end of the fourteenth grade,
the high school diploma at the end of the tenth, the elementary diploma at the end of the sixth, and if we don't
watch, we will be hurrying the baby away from the
mother's arms at age one or two and awarding a BI (bachelor of infancy) degree.

If one stops to think of it, there's nothing so grand and alluring about adulthood that we should hurry children through school to bring them into that promised land ahead of schedule. If there are potential leaders among the student body who, because of their abilities, seem to invite early promotion or the skipping of grades, the school is challenged to keep them moving with their age and maturity groups and to enrich their school experiences at all levels by enabling them to sharpen those leadership possibilities in group situations that call upon their powers. Not only they but their mates in the social and civic life of the school secure the benefits.

Just as soon as schooling is seen in its right light as something functioning for the present, it is recognized as a true part of the learner's here-and-now existence rather than merely preparation for his life ahead. Its help to his present is its greatest promise of help to his future. In this case the test of schooling becomes not so much a matter of marks and honors in subjects, but rather, how one uses his learning to improve his living with his fellows. These are true and not artificial satisfactions, whether they come at grade two or grade eleven.

7. *American society cannot afford to pay for an educational program that does not function in the here-and-now affairs of men.*

Support of public education has not come easily in America. The extent and the nature of the school program has always rested strictly upon the will of the people. This will continue to be the case. The large-city school board that deliberates at length on the increase of the annual school budget by two million dollars has as its counterpart the small town board that deliberates for an hour on the proposal to spend a hundred dollars for equipment for a kindergarten.

There comes a time when the townspeople in a small community say openly that they think the teachers are being paid enough.. Likewise, there comes a time when a city will vote more money to dispose of its sewage but no

more to build its schools, when it will spend more for buses to carry its citizens across town but no more for schools to carry its children up the socio-economic ladder.

The public not only watches with caution its expenditure for schools, but it keeps eternal vigilance over the use made of that expenditure. In the case of the lower school it continually asks first that the child be helped to read, to write, and to use numbers, and that the school take a warm, personal interest in him.

In the case of the upper school, the public must see that the work taken in the high school has made a difference for the better in the life of that student, that it has helped him with his here-and-now affairs. American society cannot afford to pay—it will not pay—for an educational program that does less.

8. *There is no conflict between the activity approach to education and the fundamentals approach.*

At times there has arisen with both educators and laymen a feeling that to approach schooling through activities is to deny the importance of certain fundamentals, or vice versa. This is hardly true. The two can support each other.

The fundamentals, as ordinarily conceived by the layman who uses the term, represent facility in (1) reading, (2) written expression, and (3) the use of numbers. The typical teacher and the typical school endorse these and add such fundamentals as facility in (1) oral expression, (2) cooperative living (democracy), (3) healthful living, (4) problem solving (thinking), and (5) wholesome recreation.

The second-grade teacher who goes all out for a six-weeks activity on dairying does not deny the goals expressed in the fundamentals mentioned above. The trip to the dairy, the visit of the milkman to the classroom, the collecting of pictures of dairy cattle from magazines, the classifying and mounting of the pictures into booklets, the development of the farm scene on the pinning board, the showing of the dairy film, and a dozen other interesting activities aid the teacher in establishing such facilities as reading, writing, using numbers, oral expression, working co-operatively, understanding health rules, solving problems, and having wholesome fun. The more formal steps in establishing these find their place in the program.

The fifth-grade teacher who builds a semester's work around a letter-writing project, in which the class members are corresponding with children in other sections of the United States, does not sacrifice reading, language study, history, and geography in the approach. Instead, such study takes on significance and meaningful interest through the joint enterprise.

The intensive research that has been done in the fields of reading, writing, and arithmetic in this century attests to the keen interest of educators in such instructional areas of long standing. It is natural for methods in teaching these subjects to have shifted with time and study.

SCHOOL AND SOCIETY

9. Complex societies call for complex schools.

The beginning teacher enters his first classroom with an extensive background of teaching experience, but it is not really his. It is that of all the teachers with whom he has come in contact in the classrooms of his own schooling, but it is experience that he is apt to use. So easily have the practices of one generation of teachers been passed on to the next that it has indeed been difficult for the beginner to do other than to take for granted nearly everything from educational goals on down to classroom questions and answers. It is so much simpler to teach as we were taught than to explore the unknown possibilities of the calling.

Acting as a force to counteract this tendency to perpetuate indefinitely a single pattern of schooling without questioning it is the constantly shifting conception of teaching and learning. This conception springs from apparent dif-

THE SOCIETY   THE SCHOOL

SPEARS

A Complex Society Calls for a Complex School

ferences in school populations and school districts, educational research and experimentation, improved training programs, and the persistent efforts of leaders in the field to keep the school in step with the general social progress. Advances in industry, science, medicine, mean advances in education.

It is pleasant to think back to the story-book conception of a true teaching situation: Mark Hopkins on one end of a log and a child on the other. But the modern American does not live in a simple world of ideas and logs. Even if the teacher wanted to escape to this humble formula of teaching, in these days of paper and pulp shortages logs are indeed scarce; and as man grapples with his problems of day-to-day existence it is quite apparent that there is no overabundance of ideas, at least no overabundance of the right ones.

It is these very problems of everyday existence that mark the teacher's job as belonging in the civic whirl of things, rather than in the quiet wood. Modern man lives in a world of intricate gadgetry, the development of which has called for the development of more intricate social and civic institutions, all of which has resulted in a world of highly complex human relationships. This is the setting for the development of the ideas and the qualities of men, the setting for the business of education.

Preparation for teaching becomes more rather than less complicated each year, not because the schools of education and the certification offices want to make it so, but because their actions reflect the ever increasing complication of American life itself. And since schools today are social institutions that serve the organized life of the people, the work of teachers must reflect directly this life that is to be advanced through such service.

A people with a simple social and economic system ask of their schools only a simple system of education, but a people with a highly complex existence must demand a much more complex system of education. The same principles of learning might serve both situations, but the same program of study or the same set of teachers' practices could not. The ever changing pattern of American education in the past three hundred years is definite proof that the people demand a school that has meaningful relationship to the advancement of their everyday affairs.

In this movement, a minority of educators and teachers have been as willing to throw away the thing that has stood the test of time and trial as have a minority of laymen been willing to yell "progressive" at any slight change from the classroom procedure they experienced thirty or forty years earlier. But, thank goodness, the great majority of teachers and educators have gracefully retained the good of the past as they open-mindedly altered the schools to serve new conditions and discoveries. And the great majority of parents have demanded and encouraged school changes just as they have stood guard over the sound practices of the past.

Topics for Study and Discussion

1. List what the public in your vicinity seem to expect of (1) the elementary school and (2) the secondary school.

2. Which of these expectations seems most reasonable?

3. Are there available for discussion any instances of the influence that one school district may have upon another, as treated in the discussion of the first principle of this chapter?

4. Principles 2 and 3 represent the two basic purposes of the American school. To what degree are these equally accepted by teachers and laymen?

5. From your observation of classroom procedures, list instances of (1) cooperative endeavor and (2) individual enterprise, as treated in principle 4.

6. In keeping with the seventh point of this chapter, which features of a typical elementary or secondary school program seem to give the taxpayers the greatest return upon their investment?

Chapter 4

Governmental Responsibility for Education

1. *As noble as they may be, the purposes of education mean nothing in themselves but are dependent upon the sound support and control of schools.*

The story of governmental responsibility for public education in America is not one of chance, but one of precept and progress, of toil and determination. The division of responsibility for a school system can be briefly summarized as follows:

1. The responsiblity for education in America rests with the respective states, since no provision was made in the Federal Constitution. The Tenth Amendment reads: "The powers not delegated to the United States by the Constitution, nor prohibited by it to the states, are reserved to the states respectively, or to the people."

2. The financial support for the schools in most states still comes largely from local sources, but the percentage of the total coming from state revenue has been increasing in the past quarter of a century.

3. Although in a legal sense public education is a state

JUST AN OLD AMERICAN CUSTOM

responsibility, control of the schools is left largely to the local community. For instance, a teacher must meet state requirements to secure a teaching credential, but once on the job he turns to local authorities for direction.

4. The Federal government gives financial support to some few special types of educational programs, such as vocational training for agriculture, trades and industries, home-making, and distributive occupations.

The earliest advocates of the American republic realized that the success of the young government and its later perpetuation, as well, were dependent upon a system of education that would bring the citizens up to the level of literacy and civic action implied in a government that was to derive its just powers from the consent of the governed. In turning its back upon a system of government that endorsed the appointment of leadership from the classes and in turning to one that was to derive its leaders from the masses, the young nation challenged the respective states to underwrite this noble action by providing in their constitutions for state systems of public education.

State School Systems. The study of the provisions for education in the state constitutions and in the school laws invoked by state legislatures is a study in itself. A graduate student of education, working for a master's degree or a doctorate, would indeed find such an investigation highly enlightening.

The legislature shall provide for the maintenance and support of a system of free common schools, wherein all the children of this state may be educated—is a typical statement from a state constitution, this one from New York, vesting the legislature with the responsibility of seeing to it that ALL the children receive a free education.

And so, American public education springs from—	The American Democratic Way of Life
Education specifically provided for in a—	State Constitution
The state constitution passes the responsibility to the—	State Legislature
The state legislature in turn provides for a—	State Board of Education
And also a—	State Department of Public Instruction
Headed by a chief school officer called State Commissioner of Education or—	State Superintendent of Public Instruction
Who gives educational leadership with the aid of a—	State School Staff
Working quite independently but subject to state regulations is the—	Local Board of Education

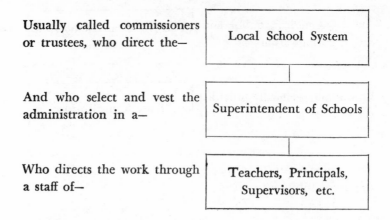

Usually called commissioners or trustees, who direct the— | Local School System

And who select and vest the administration in a— | Superintendent of Schools

Who directs the work through a staff of— | Teachers, Principals, Supervisors, etc.

History and Heroics. The local school system is accountable to the state department of public instruction for providing a school program in keeping with the constitutional and legislative requirements. These regulations deal with teacher certification, financing the schools, the organization of school boards, the curriculum of the schools, building and safety regulations, and a score of other matters.

Only as he advances in the profession and in experience and study can the teacher hope to understand fully the sensitive maze of inter-relationships represented by the national, state, and local factors in school organization, administration, and control. The democratic emphasis that exists here and there in this network of controls has behind it a heroic as well as a historical story.

THE SUPPORT AND CONTROL OF EARLY SCHOOLS

The story of the American school system is over three hundred years old—a courageous, militant, forward looking account that cannot be dismissed with the few paragraphs or pages to be included here. It is punctuated with the efforts of Thomas Jefferson, Horace Mann, Caleb Mills, Henry Barnard, Calvin Wiley, and a host of other American leaders who envisioned the close relationship of the development of a nation and a public school system.

At one end of the struggle was a man such as Governor Berkeley of the colony of Virginia, who in 1671 thanked God that there were no free schools and no printing presses in Virginia, and expressed the hope that there would be none for a hundred years. At the other end was a man such as Thomas Jefferson, who a hundred years or so later, in the state of Virginia, stated: "If a nation expects to be ignorant and free in a state of civilization it expects what never will be. . . . There is no safe deposit [for the functions of government] but with the people themselves; nor can they be safe with them without information."

—And John Adams said: "The whole people must take upon themselves the education of the whole people and be willing to bear the expense of it."

—And James Madison, who in 1787 pointed out: "Above all things, I hope the education of the common people will be attended to; convinced that on this good sense we may rely with the most security for the preservation of a due sense of liberty."

—And Horace Mann, who in dispelling the doubts held by an opponent of adequate schools, said: "There are owls who, to adapt the world to their own eyes, would always keep the sun from rising."

One should apologize for any insinuation in the inclusion of this short historical section that grasping the true import of these early beginnings of our schools is that simple. It isn't. It demands the careful study of any teacher, and it challenges the further search of the graduate student for true interpretation. The few references that follow are enough to establish these truths:

2. *The fight to defend the proper support of public education today is just as essential as was yesterday's fight to achieve it.*

3. *The good that is to be achieved from a public school is for the community or the society in general as well as for the child being educated.*

The latter, now a commonly accepted principle of school provision, is just as plainly stated in this quotation from a famous Massachusetts law of 1642 as it is stated in any twentieth century state school law:

> Forasmuch as the good education of children is of singular behoofe and benefit to any Commonwealth, & whereas many parents & masters are too indulgent of their duty in that kind, It is Ordered that the Select Men of every Town in the several precincts, and quarters where they dwel, shall have a vigilant eye over their brethren and neighbors to see, first that none of them shall suffer so much barbarism in any of their families, as not to endeavor to teach, by themselves or others, their children & apprentices, so much learning, as may enable them to perfectly read the English tongue, and knowledge of the Capital laws; upon penaltie of twenty shillings for each neglect therein.

These early civic leaders were not willing to leave it to either parent or master of apprentices to educate a child. They placed the responsibility squarely upon the community as a whole "forasmuch as the good education of children is of singular behoofe and benefit to any Commonwealth." In fact, they were stating this principle of the American school system:

4. *The welfare of the state is so dependent upon the education of each child that it is the state's responsibility to hold parents to their obligation in the matter.*

This Massachusetts statute represented the first time in the history of English-speaking peoples that a legislative body representing the State ordered that all the children should be taught to read. Five years later there came another law that likewise had no precedent in the English-speaking world. Following closely upon the highly significant 1642 legislation was the Massachusetts school law of 1647, passed by the General Court, which included this mandate:

It is therefore ordered, That every township in this jurisdiction, after the Lord hath increased it to the number of fifty householders, shall then forthwith appoint one within their towne to teach all such children as shall report to him to write and reade, whose wages shall be paid either by the parents or master of such children, or by the inhabitants in generall, by way of supply, as the major part of those that order the prudentials of the towne shall appoint; Provided, Those that send their children be not oppressed by paying much more than they can have them taught for in their other townes; and it is further ordered, That where any towne shall increase to the number of one hundred families or householders, they shall set up a grammar schoole, the master thereof being able to instruct youth so farr as they may be fited for the University; Provided That if any towne neglect the performance hereof above one yeare, that every such towne shall pay 5£ to the next schoole till they shall performe this order.

Of course, in any community today there is still the minority element, the tax reductionist who would question why he should support schools when he has no children of his own to benefit therefrom. Adequate school support has never come easily and, as the records show, has been fought for every inch of the way from colonial New England down to the present. There is a story that in the early days a Vermont aristocrat who purchased private education for his own children asked his neighbor Thaddeus Stevens why one should be asked to pay for public schools when he wasn't going to use them himself. Neighbor Stevens replied, "I trust it is not your intention to use the public jails you support either?"

This Massachusetts law of 1647 expressed almost as clearly as it could be expressed in today's legislation for public school support, the principle that:

5. *The responsibility for the support of the American common school system shall rest upon the people as a whole rather than upon the parents of the children being educated.*

ELEMENTARY SCHOOLING

This dogged determination of colonial leaders to provide schools for all children does not mean that a New England town school was the free school as we know it today. In fact, the strong influence of religious thought over the state indicated that this intense interest in teaching all to read was pointed toward reading the Bible. However, the religious motive is insignificant when compared with the influence of the 1642 and 1647 laws in helping to set a later pattern of.public support for schools in the nation. The responsibility for seeing that all children were educated was vested in the state by the 1642 law, and the support of the education was vested in the state by the 1647 law. Connecticut passed a law in 1650 similar to these two. And since Massachusetts then included what is now New Hampshire and Vermont, most of New England endorsed these principles of school support and control.

Needless to say, every colonial town did not have a school, in spite of the regulations. Much of the responsibility for teaching reading and religion was assumed by parents in their homes and by the masters of the apprentices, the system of apprenticeship having been established early in New England. When schools were established and schoolmasters had to be paid, perhaps the parents did pay fees to supplement the public endowment, but nevertheless the principle of public obligation for education found a footing in American life. It was not something transplanted from Mother England, for there education was still the responsibility of parents alone.

These New England settlers deserve little credit for interest in the rights of men or children. By chance children in general benefited by this expression of the public will, but only by chance. The colonial leaders were more interested in religion than children.. The advancement of the idea of the right to life, liberty, and the pursuit of happiness had to await a later period in American life.

Popular education of the citizen for his own advancement was not in the thinking of these colonists.

Regardless of the motives behind this intense interest of the New England state in schooling for its children, it stands out as the bright spot in all colonial school practice. Only there were planted the seeds of public control and support of education as we know it today. In all other

MASSACHUSETTS
COLONY

PUBLIC
SUPPORT
OF
SCHOOLS

THE FIRST PLANTING

sections of colonial America education was private schooling, with churches assuming a major role. The clergymen were usually the teachers of the parochial schools. The public interest in schools was usually limited to providing rudimentary instruction to poor children. Thus, in most places outside of New England the public school was not to lose its pauper-school taint until the nineteenth century. The idea of the common school to serve state ends rather than church ends was to find its big impetus then.

The early schools, regardless of how supported, offered a meager curriculum of reading and religion, with occasionally some attention to counting, spelling, and writing. Not until after the Revolutionary War was arithmetic to take its prominent place in the curriculum. The scarcity of instructional materials such as paper restricted the program, even discouraging the teaching of writing. The various ages and levels of instruction represented in these one-teacher schools, coupled with limited materials and teaching ability, resulted in one pattern of classroom operation. The teacher would call each child to his desk individually to have him recite his lesson. This plus physical punishment just about constituted the teacher's kit of teaching techniques.

Discipline was severe, reflecting not only the attitude toward children expressed in the home, but also the practical aspects of the classroom situation. With a roomful of children of all ages, having little to do while awaiting their turn to recite individually at the teacher's desk, and with the art of silent reading still somewhat far removed for most of the children, the schoolmaster indeed faced a real problem in keeping order. Expressing the mood as well as the melody of the early American classroom, Elsbree, in *The American Teacher* resurrects this early poem by John Trumbull:

Progress of Dulness

> He tries with ease and unconcern,
> To teach what ne'er himself could learn;
> Gives law and punishment alone,
> Judge, jury, bailiff, all in one;
> Holds all good learning must depend

Upon his rod's extremist end,
Whose great electric virtue's such,
Each genius brightens at the touch;
With threats and blows, excitements pressing,
Drives on his lads to learn each lesson;
Thinks flogging cures all moral ills,
And breaks their heads to break their wills.[1]

In contrast, the easy manner of the teacher in today's classroom and the minimum of confusion in spite of the absence of severity reflect the enriched and meaningful program, the fine training given teachers, the excellent materials and supplies, and the strength of good supervision and administration.

SECONDARY SCHOOLING

The Latin Grammar School. In brief, the story of American secondary education is the account of three schools with three almost distinct and consecutive periods of influence: the Latin Grammar School, the Academy, and the High School. Theirs is the story of the struggle between two ideas, the one that the secondary school should be a selective institution for those able to pay the bills—for those of certain interests, and the other that it should be an extension of the free public common school, open to all the children of all the people. The idea of a public institution started slowly in the colonial period, ran a poor second from the Revolutionary War until the Kalamazoo decision in 1874, and since then has outdistanced the field.

---

[1] Willard Elsbree, *The American Teacher*, New York: American Book Company, 1939, pp. 33-34.

It is not strange that to Massachusetts goes the credit for the first secondary school in America, for it came as a part of the thinking behind the 1642 and 1647 laws mentioned above. As the colony demanded every town of 50 families to maintain a common school, it doubled this quota for the next higher school, the grammar school.

The Boston Latin School, opened in 1635, was the first of these, its purpose being to prepare boys for Harvard College. These Latin Grammar schools, long on college influence and short on curriculum, limped along through the first half of the eighteenth century and for the most part disappeared from the American scene by the end of the Revolutionary War. They were copied from European models and were never adjusted to fit the unique characteristics of life in the new country. Consequently, they disappeared by 1800. They established for later American use the fact that the public could support secondary schools as well as elementary schools. Their crowning achievement was their means of support, which was public.

The Academy. For the next hundred years or so, the history of American secondary education was largely one of private education. It was the story of the private academy. From the establishment of Benjamin Franklin's *Publick Academy in the City of Philadelphia,* in 1751, down to the famous Kalamazoo Case in 1874, the private academies thrived and almost killed the idea of public supported secondary schools. Some academies were supported in part or in whole by towns, but most of them charged entrance fees and were commonly backed by religious groups or private endowments.

Although the public-spirited Franklin had intended the academy to serve first the interests of the growing middle class, and second the preparation for college, within fifty years the two purposes had been reversed in the scheme of things. In its heyday the academy never did represent a definite sequence of grades as does the public high school or the private academy today. Although one academy of the past century drew youth between ages 13 and 17, another served a range from 8 to 18, and so on. The relatively few academies that exist today are private and in purpose are usually set up as college preparatory schools.

The Public High School. In 1821, a full half century before the academy reached the peak of its glory, another type of secondary school was founded, the English Classical School. Instigated by the mercantile and mechanic classes wanting a school more useful than the typical academy, this new school was soon renamed the English High School. Later the word English was dropped.

Insignificant as it was in its original emergence upon the American educational horizon, within a half century this school was to prove to be the pot of free secondary education at the end of the equality-of-opportunity rainbow. Its birth and development during the past century were just as natural a part of that century's extension of American democracy as was the sweep of homesteaders from one coast to the other. In other words, its coming was not by chance. It was born of the spirit of American freedom and opportunity, of the search for equality among men.

The planners geared the age range more nearly to the adolescent years than did the academy, that it might fit onto the common school rather than overlap it. The number of high schools in 1860 was 40, in 1870 about 160, in 1880 it jumped to 800, in 1890 to 2500, and by 1900 it reached 6000.

The Kalamazoo Case. It was the famous Kalamazoo Case of 1874 that marked the official blessing of the school as the legalized extension of the public common school, the court decision that made it lawful for people to tax themselves to support a local school above the eight-grade common school if they so desired. Before that case, brought as a test by the school board of Kalamazoo, Michigan, no state had known if it were legal to consider the common school to run above the eighth grade and thus to support it publicly.

6. *The legalization of the free public high school by the courts can well be considered the most significant incident in the development of American secondary education.*

The Graded System. Today, any community in America presents a clean-cut system of schooling, with a full elementary school, extending neatly into a secondary school, which in turn fits into the state colleges or university. At times a kindergarten program is provided, from which the child moves directly into the first grade of the elementary school. In other words, this is the graded system of education, with no overlapping of institutions and consequently no lost motion. This is the product of American educational ingenuity, for until 1850 the country specialized in ungraded institutions that overlapped in function as well as in age levels served. The various school systems over the country differ in the place they make their institutional breaks in this ladder of schooling, but in any case the different parts fit neatly into a continuous pattern of schooling. The usual patterns of organization of school systems are indicated in Figure 3.

EQUALITY OF EDUCATIONAL OPPORTUNITY

To conclude that America has achieved equality of educational opportunity would be foolish. The history of American education is a story of progressively greater equality of opportunity, but that history is not concluded.

7. *The principle of equality of educational opportunity is best served when each teacher puts it to practice in his own classroom.*

The right of each child to free schooling is just as truly a principle of the American way of life as are the rights to "life, liberty, and the pursuit of happiness." By the early years of 1800, so commonly accepted was the idea that all people—not just the privileged—had equal rights

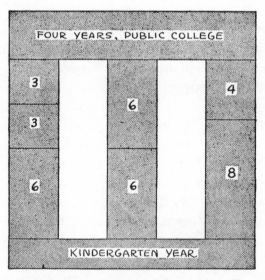

FIG. 3. ORGANIZATIONAL PATTERNS COMMONLY FOLLOWED IN SCHOOL SYSTEMS

and opportunities to fame and fortune, that it followed naturally that free schooling was to become one of the rather well-marked highways to this goal. It made little difference in those early days that school membership was skimpy. The important thing was the feeling of democratic satisfaction that came to a man when he knew his children had just as much right in the local school as did those of his neighbor on the hill. Even though he may not

have gotten around to sending them, the knowledge that he had the right to do so gave him a feeling of equality.

For the young teacher who steps into the classroom for the first time and looks over the roomful of children, it is well to remember that each of these boys and girls, regardless of first impressions, has an American right to be there. It is not his appearance or his ability that is the point in question; it is that his presence represents the implementation of this basic principle of American life—*equality of opportunity*. If a teacher, in disgust, asked a child why he is going to school, were the child profound he might well reply, "The state constitution grants me that right." Yes, as stated in the New York code, "the legislature shall provide for the maintenance and support of a system of free common schools, wherein all the children of this state may be educated," a principle found in all state governments. The doors of the public school stand open for all the children, and it is our responsibility to continue to seek the best methods possible of fulfilling our obligation to the American way of life.

Free tuition to a public school is coupled in many states with free textbooks, free transportation, dental and medical inspection and sometimes care, special classes for the handicapped, varied courses, and what-not in respect of the fact that all boys and girls are of equal worth. As he progresses in the profession, it will become more and more evident to the teacher that the American Constitution gives no special privileges to any one class or interest and that the public school can follow no better ideal.

Constantly at work all over the nation are forces that tend to equalize the educational offering. Some of these have to do with distributing the school funds more equally, and others have to do with broadening or adjusting the curriculum to see that all children are served to a maximum.

State Support of Schools. For some years there has been a growing tendency for more of the support of local schools to come from state sources. To collect school money on a statewide basis and to redistribute it more equitably among the local school units is in keeping with America's ideal of equality of opportunity. For the country as a whole, last available statistics indicated that the ratio of state support to local support in school revenue stood: 38.9 per cent from the state, 2.8 per cent from Federal money, and 58.3 per cent from the local and county school funds. Fifteen years ago, only 20 per cent of the funds came from state sources of revenue.

Just as the responsibility for public schooling is a state matter, so is this matter of how schools shall be financed. The variation in ratio of state to local revenue is indeed as broad as the geographical distance between the states. For instance, in Delaware and New Mexico over 85 per cent of local school costs are paid by the state, but in Iowa and Massachusetts the state pays less than 15 per cent of the bill. (See Table 5.)

TABLE 5

Variation in the Support of Public Schools [2]

	Source of Revenue, by Percentages			Spent per Pupil
	Federal	State	Local & County	
United States	2.8%	38.9%	58.3%	$179
NEW ENGLAND	1.9	18.2	79.9	201
Maine	2.3	26.8	70.9	133
New Hampshire	2.6	17.0	80.4	187
Vermont	3.6	25.5	70.9	167
Massachusetts	1.4	12.6	86.0	214
Rhode Island	2.1	19.4	78.5	221
Connecticut	2.2	24.8	73.0	217

2 U. S. Office of Education statistics, March, 1950, for year 1947-48.

TABLE 5—*Continued*

| | Source of Revenue, by Percentages | | | Spent per Pupil |
	Federal	State	Local & County	
MIDDLE ATLANTIC	1.1%	30.8%	68.1%	$228
New York	1.0	32.6	66.4	257
New Jersey	1.1	16.2	82.7	251
Pennsylvania	1.1	35.9	63.0	184
EAST NORTH CENTRAL.	1.8	34.2	64.0	205
Ohio	1.3	39.6	59.1	192
Indiana	1.5	39.6	58.9	217
Illinois	2.3	15.9	81.8	223
Michigan	1.9	54.5	43.6	198
Wisconsin	2.3	19.6	78.1	191
WEST NORTH CENTRAL	1.8	23.6	74.6	187
Minnesota	1.8	37.4	60.8	213
Iowa	1.6	13.9	84.5	189
Missouri	2.1	34.4	63.5	164
North Dakota	1.6	26.3	72.1	182
South Dakota	1.0	17.5	81.5	194
Nebraska	1.9	5.5	92.6	181
Kansas	1.6	11.4	87.0	191
SOUTH ATLANTIC	5.3	54.2	30.5	131
Delaware	3.0	86.4	10.6	204
Maryland	2.6	40.7	56.7	193
Dist. Columbia	0.7	14.3	85.0	219
Virginia	4.2	42.8	53.0	125
West Virginia	4.8	64.0	31.2	142
North Carolina	9.0	66.2	24.8	109

TABLE 5—*Continued*

| | Source of Revenue, by Percentages | | | Spent per Pupil |
	Federal	State	Local & County	
South Carolina	8.3%	60.7%	31.0%	$112
Georgia	5.8	57.9	36.2	104
Florida	3.0	52.8	44.2	161
EAST SOUTH CENTRAL.	8.7	55.0	36.3	100
Kentucky	8.3	42.1	49.6	112
Tennessee	12.8	51.7	35.5	108
Alabama	4.9	72.8	22.3	106
Mississippi	6.9	50.8	42.3	71
WEST SOUTH CENTRAL.	5.8	52.8	41.4	146
Arkansas	6.5	62.7	30.8	93
Louisiana	8.8	60.9	30.3	145
Oklahoma	3.2	50.1	46.7	144
Texas	5.6	50.0	44.4	165
MOUNTAIN	2.8	37.1	60.1	193
Montana	3.2	17.8	79.0	247
Idaho	2.0	23.6	74.4	163
Wyoming	3.9	29.6	66.5	195
Colorado	1.5	20.8	77.7	188
New Mexico	2.2	87.5	10.3	186
Arizona	2.8	46.4	50.8	204
Utah	4.2	45.5	50.3	180
Nevada	7.0	37.1	55.9	231
PACIFIC	1.4	49.2	49.4	217
Washington	1.8	62.7	35.5	237
Oregon	1.1	35.0	63.9	217
California	1.3	47.5	51.2	212

For the child who happens to live in New York or New Jersey, approximately 150 per cent more money is spent on his education each year than is spent on that of the child who happens to live in Georgia or Alabama. Three times as much is spent on the child in Illinois as on the one in Mississippi. In other words:

8. *The standard of schooling offered in a state is reflected by the amount of money spent per pupil.*

ADA: Average Daily Attendance. The young teacher is at times perplexed, almost irked, by the detailed reports of attendance that have to be made out for each class. This is not mere busywork; it represents an essential cog in the financial machinery that brings state revenue to the local school district. In school accounting, it was long ago discovered that the significant figure is not the number of children enrolled on the school registers but the number who actually attend.

And so, *average daily attendance* has become the key in the state's distribution of school revenue on the basis of children served. In school terminology, this has been shortened to ADA and the periods dropped. And so in a school district served by state aid, the attendance of Johnny or Mary on October 17, March 3, or any other day in the school calendar bears an actual dollar-and-cents value to the local district.

Years of Schooling. A comparison of the years people spend in school likewise reveals differences in schooling by states. To answer the question, *How many years make up the common schooling,* one must limit himself neither to the public concept of what a person needs nor to the state statutes that set down the compulsory attendance laws. Rather, he needs to turn to the statistics telling what the average citizen actually secures in the way of schooling.

The U. S. Bureau of Census, Department of Commerce, includes in its statistics a tabulation of the median years of school completed by persons twenty-five years old and over, believing that in ordinary times a person will have completed his schooling by age twenty-five. The data in this table bring out the chance of birth as a pronounced factor in the amount of schooling a person might be expected to secure. For instance, Utah residents average 10.2 years of schooling as compared with 6.7 years for South Carolina residents or over 50 per cent more schooling. The median years of school completed by native whites in South Carolina is 8.7 as contrasted with 3.9 for Negroes, or 125 per cent more schooling. In California, the range between the two is not nearly so wide: 10.8 for the native white and 8.3 for the Negro. This 8.3 is greater than the median for all residents in three of the state groups, South Atlantic, East South Central, and West South Central.

For the country as a whole, the median years of schooling completed is 8.4, with this break-down by groups: native white 8.8, foreign-born white 7.3, Negro 5.7, and other races 6.8. The figure for urban sections is 8.7 as contrasted to 7.7 for farming sections.

The variation among sections of the country is: New England 8.8, Middle Atlantic 8.4, East North Central 8.5, West North Central 8.5, South Atlantic 7.8, East South Central 7.5, West South Central 8.1, Mountain 8.9, and Pacific 9.7.

9. *The educational opportunities offered by a state can be measured to a marked degree by the average number of years that the citizens have spent in the schools.*

One studying the situation appreciates that the problem of extending public education in the present less-privileged sections of our country reflects the economic and social problems of those sections rather than the desire of educational and civic leaders to do a better job.

Federal Support of Education. As indicated above, public education is a state responsibility; to date, not only the control but the support of the program has been kept within the states' lines. As a state moved in the direction of providing a greater part of school money from state revenue, there was the assurance that control would still rest with the local community.

For years there has been a concerted effort to have the Federal government assume more of the responsibility for the support of the common schools. It was pointed out that the equality-of-opportunity principle of American life cannot be served adequately when there is so much variation among the states in their ability to support a school program. (See Table 5.)

The educators who have opposed Federal aid to education have done so on grounds that with Federal support of education is bound to come Federal control, through bureaucracy, killing off local interest, which has been the fountainhead of the American public school system. Statesmen who have opposed Federal support point out the danger of discouraging individual initiative and enterprise, which have been major factors in the development of our nation. The controversy that has been waged over

the issue of Federal aid to schools has found educators as
well as congressmen in different camps.

Since the First World War, the Federal government has
provided funds for vocational education in secondary
schools. It was reasoned that this program, calling for a

HAROLD
SPEARS

WITH SUPPORT GOES CONTROL

great outlay of equipment and also for classes much
smaller than the typical academic course, presented a
financial burden that discouraged the local district's provision of such a program. Therefore, the Federal government voted money for the program, distributing it through

the respective state departments of public instruction, thus assuring local control and management. These funds constitute about twelve million dollars a year and provide for agricultural education, trade and industrial courses, home economics programs, distributive occupations courses, and teacher training in these areas.

To qualify for this money, a local school must set up its vocational courses on the time-and-offering pattern set down in the regulations. In general, approximately half of the instructor's salary comes from Federal money and half from the usual revenue of the local school.

Public and Private Schools

The history of American education reflects two different principles of school organization, support, and control, namely, (1) public education and (2) private education. Paralleling the free public school, tax supported and open to all children and youth, has been the private school, open to those admitted in keeping with the particular interest represented by the private support and control. Private schools in general are of two types. Situated especially in the larger cities is the parochial school, supported and controlled by a church. Part of the support of the school comes from the church, and part from tuition fees paid by the families whose children are accepted. The great majority of church schools are day schools but at times they are boarding schools.

The other type of private school is supported through private ownership; it may be either a day school or a boarding school. These schools for the most part appeal to the families of the upper economic level, and most of the support of the school comes from the fees paid by the pupils' families. Because of these tuition fees, enrollments in these schools fluctuate to a degree with the variations in the economic condition of the country. Often this type of private school makes its reputation as a preparatory school, gearing its curriculum to college entrance. In the East it is common for the school to specialize in entrance to a specific private college, such as Harvard or Princeton.

As to comparative enrollments, at the elementary-school level in America there are sixteen public schools to one private, and for each child in a private school there are eight in a public school. At the high-school level there are eight public schools to one private, and for each child in a private secondary school there are ten in a public school.

The ratio of private to public schools varies greatly in different sections of the country. For instance, in Wyoming, a state born of the equality-of-opportunity spirit of the American frontier, last available statistics reveal that there are only 7 private elementary schools to 646 public, and only one private secondary school as contrasted with 98 public high schools. In Massachusetts, in a section of the country where educational practice has been greatly influenced by the old private colleges and where large cities present church schools, the ratio is 401 private elementary schools to 1771 public, and 202 private secondary to 428 public.

Nevada, another state born of the frontier, has only one private high school to 38 public, and only one private elementary school to 201 public. Connecticut's ratio is 76 private to 125 public secondary schools, and 189 private to 772 public elementary schools.

It is possible for the curriculum of a private school to be narrower than that of a public school since it restricts its student body in keeping with the particular interest being served. It can function with a more restrictive program since it has complete control over the entrance and dismissal of its pupils. On the other hand, the public school, born of the principle of equality of opportunity, opens its doors to all the children of all the people. The broadening of the program of the public school according to the varied differences among children reflects the democratic principles on which public education was founded.

History of Public-school Support. The idea of a free public school, tax-supported and just around the corner for each American child regardless of race, religion, or economic standing, was not achieved overnight. It has been won by lay and professional leaders who have recognized education as a function of the state, calling for a public-school system good enough for all and adequate to meet the needs of all our citizens.

The public's right to tax itself to support an eight-year elementary school, called the common school, was accepted in the early days of our nation. But, as noted above, not until Michigan's famous Kalamazoo Case of 1874 was it determined by the courts that a community could tax itself to support a high school. Until that time there had been waged in the nation an intensive struggle to determine if America's leading high school was to be set up along private or public lines. Today any citizen is assured that just around the corner or at the end of the free school-bus line, there is a common school for his children, the common school extending at least through high-school graduation.

Where this picture, as just described, is dimmed a bit

by limitations, by and large they are not limitations of the noble ideal of American democracy, but rather limitations in finding the means to implement the ideal.

Topics for Study and Discussion

1. What actual contacts does the State Department of Public Instruction make with local schools in this state in keeping with its responsibility for schooling throughout the state?

2. Are there instances of citizens today being as devoted to the idea of public education as were the early leaders of our country?

3. What obligation does a local school district place upon parents in regard to the education of their children?

4. Account for the fact that New England supplied so much of the impetus for the early development of the idea of an adequate system of education in America.

5. What are the rights to schooling that the children of various ages possess in this state? in this locality?

6. Check the principle of equality of educational opportunity as applied in this state and in this locality.

7. Secure from the Bureau of the Census, Department of Commerce, the latest table giving the years of schooling completed by persons 25 years old and over. Use this for comparing local conditions with conditions in other sections of the country.

PART II

Teaching—*From the Position of the Pupil*

Chapter 5

The Will and the Way to Learn

NO BEGINNING TEACHER IS EXPECTED TO ENTER THE CLASS-
room with a complete knowledge and understanding of
educational psychology. However, he should have given
some careful consideration to this matter of how children
learn, so that he may enter that first classroom with a fair
appreciation of the learning possibilities.

The study of methods and techniques of teaching must
not be confused as a study of the learning process. Methods and techniques refer to what the teacher does to set
up a learning situation and to carry out his part. The
learning process refers to what the child goes through in
learning. A good teacher's manual that accompanies a
basic set of readers treats the teacher's techniques of teaching reading. However, if it is good, the author has based
the suggested procedures on a sound knowledge of the
learning process. It then stands to reason that the more
the teacher understands the learning process, the more
readily he will master the techniques explained in the
manual.

Learning deals with getting and expressing ideas. On
the surface, how children learn seems simple. They ob-

serve, they read, they imitate, they try something them-selves, they listen, they follow directions. But behind these surface symptoms is an intricate and broad field of study of human behavior. The principles that are treated in this chapter are but a few of the summary statements of that field.

THE PSYCHOLOGY OF TEACHING

1. *Good teaching is a matter of drawing-out rather than a matter of putting-in.*

Psychology has not yet told us exactly how learning takes place, and we cannot wait for the perfect answer—school must go on. However, it is assured that learning is an active thing, that it comes from within, and that it is achieved through the learner's doing something about or with his surroundings: people and things. The teacher and the instructional materials form an important part of these surroundings.

This all goes to say that we don't give learning to a child; we promote it with him. We don't pound education into him; we draw it out. Effective learning asks that the child accept purposes and make the effort himself, the teacher helping to direct the activity that will lead him to his goals. Any "intake" is dependent upon the child's action, the teacher aiding and encouraging. In the proc-ess the results that are achieved, be they skill in reading or a drawing rich with color and design, reflect the unique nature of the learner, the something that has come from him alone.

A teacher, in establishing competence with numbers, may make the assignment of some problems or exercises, but the practice with them comes from the pupil, who establishes learning through his efforts. The teacher has set up the situation and guides the process, which is teaching. But the learning comes from the pupil and reflects his unique nature.

Teaching, then, must be appreciated as much harder than assigning something "to learn." Determining the possibilities for learning inherent in each child, setting the stage to bring forth each talent and each skill, and taking advantage of the group situation of the classroom without permitting it to react against the development of any one child, all these are a part of the skill exercised by a good teacher.

To determine the combination of events and factors that will excite the child to respond to the fullest measure, to put his best foot foremost, this is the challenge that teachers face in setting the stage of a learning situation.

2. *Learning is an active and not a passive process.*

Children are busy people. Their lives are full of many things, important things. They are active. They are improving their ways of doing things. They are learning as they are doing.

The school does not give the child his education. He can never receive it in this passive manner. But a school can set up the situation so that through his own activity the child can learn.

When "telling time" opens the day in the first grade, Henry will profit most by coming from his chair to the front of the group and telling the important thing that happened to him on the way to school. Learning to express himself with assurance before the group cannot come from sitting passively in his chair throughout the period, anymore than ability to swim can come to his older brother without getting into the water.

"Let me do it" is the universal demand of young children as they watch their mothers or fathers doing something that looks interesting to them. It may be pounding a nail, sweeping the floor, or even reading words on a page. The child who first walks by holding the hand of the father, finally shakes loose from the support, as if to say, "Let me do it alone, daddy."

TEACHING FOR DEMOCRACY

3. *In preparing for citizenship, teaching about democracy isn't nearly as effective as teaching through democratic procedure.*

Since a person learns by doing, the school must provide practice in, as well as knowledge of, democratic living. State legislators in most states have placed in the statutes mandates requiring the teaching of American history and American government. Had these legislators been aware of what the educational profession knows about how learning takes place, they would have coupled such legislation with the requirement that schools provide practice in democratic living.

Free speech, free press, the right of discussion and criticism, the appreciation of the rights of others, the rule of the majority, the worth of the individual in American life, and dozens of other principles of American democracy can be read and recited in a classroom, but they can be

DIFFERENTIATED CURRICULA
ELECTIONS
MANAGING ONE'S SELF
OPINIONS OF ALL
COOPERATIVE ACTION
RESPECT FOR IN
A
C
Y

SPEARS

firmly rooted in the lives of school children only if those children are given the chance to practice the principles in the planned life of the school. Chance situations are not enough.

Through actual practice in classroom and other school situations the pupil best comes to appreciate democracy. The teacher who wishes to teach democracy must first see that his own procedures respect the principles that he would strengthen with his pupils. Sharing the planning with the pupils, respecting the worth of each child, and using classroom methods that require co-operative action of the pupils are but a few of the steps toward democracy open to any teacher.

4. *Co-operation is a complicated and essential social tool of democracy, the use of which must be taught rather than left to chance or trial and error.*

It is common for the school's home report card to carry a list of citizenship traits to be rated by the teacher, one of which invariably is co-operation. However, it is not so common for the school to give systematic training in this fine art of democratic living. Especially is the subject-centered high school lax in this respect.

A high school often takes the liberty to mark a student on this quality without giving the training systematically. For instance, a history teacher may limit his efforts at teaching citizenship to the content of his subject and rate the student's co-operation on the basis of his overt reactions to the course requirements.

In teaching children to co-operate for the common good, teachers must take advantage of group situations that they set up for the purpose. For instance, one teacher may be handling his civics class of 30 in five groups of six students each. The techniques of group action, involving the responsibility of the individual to the group and the group to the individual, are carefully discussed and established. Parallel situations in history or out-of-school community life are used as examples. Assignments in the class are often handled by the five groups rather than by all pupils as individuals. The give-and-take of the six members of a committee and their sharing of responsibilities means much to this teacher in his effort to sharpen his pupils' appreciation of co-operation. As the five class groups merge their projects and reports into a whole-class enterprise, again co-operative techniques come to the front.

Co-operation is not something to be taken for granted by schools. It is a significant social tool calling for careful teaching and practice in its use under the direction of the school.

5. *The learner cannot be considered aside from his environment.*

He always has his feet mired in his own particular environment. Some of its elements are common to the soil of the others in the class, but many of the features are peculiar to his world alone.

It is true that the twenty-eight students before you have in common the subject that brings them together, but they have "in uncommon" their varied backgrounds. A father whose work takes him from home days at a time, a troublesome complexion, an exceptionally high reading ability, a divorced home, a close friend, a mother working, a before-school paper route, sole ownership of a sports roadster, membership in a clique, a feeling of insecurity, and a hundred and one other personal distinctions have their bearing on the classroom assignment. An assignment in history or arithmetic means twenty-eight different things

to twenty-eight different class members, so naturally it cannot mean just one thing to the teacher.

Environment is not a cloak that is shed upon entrance to the school house. It is the mud on our feet that we carry around with us, the mud that we can't shake off. It would be a waste of paper to belabor the point that the more you know your students, the greater the teaching advantage you hold.

THE LEARNER'S UNIQUE POSITION

6. *Personality plays a great part in life.*

You must not discount personality in the classroom. It is history by now that some years ago an intensive New York Regents survey of the school practices of that state

revealed that by and large school teachers minimize personality and the business and social worlds capitalize upon it and that, whether we like it or not, personal impressions made by boys and girls who apply for jobs weigh more heavily than school records.

Remember that the person in front of you in the class is first a personality and second a student of the thing you are trying to teach. If there is any doubt in your mind about this, just note how a particular little Flossie in the group releases with ease the pent-up kittenish antics of the boy next to her. As a teacher of a subject, it may be difficult for you at times to remember that this action is more essential to the perpetuation of the race than the assignment for the day. At least it should be no shock to the biology teacher.

If we are inclined to overlook the personality factor, perhaps it is a result of the fact that so many of our traditional pedagogical procedures deal with judging and grad-

ing children in their mastery of facts and skills, and as teachers who want to be fair we lean over backwards to be on guard against the student who would "polish the apple" or "turn on his personality" to secure a standing in the teacher's eyes that is above his actual scholastic performance. Out in life, gray matter, personality, and effort are all three rolled into one, and perhaps only in academic institutions do we try to break them apart.

7. *The student who is learning is working for himself rather than for the teacher.*

Schooling should not be a matter of children performing for teachers. Psychologically it could better be conceived

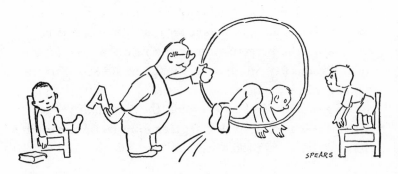

of as teachers working for children, and children for themselves. The teacher who has a deep interest in her students indeed works diligently for them as she sets the stage for learning.

It is human nature for a person to desire approval of his accomplishment from one whom he respects. It is natural for a child to look to a teacher for this commendation, but the work itself must reflect his own purposes and represent intrinsic benefits to him. His learning satisfactions must be deeper than pleasing the teacher.

If students are to be permitted to work for themselves, the classroom cannot be geared to a teacher's stop-and-go signal, with activity beginning with her assignment and stopping abruptly at its completion until she assigns something else that she wants done. Under this system even the brighter students lose initiative and are soon conditioned to await the teacher's order before going beyond the assignment. It is relatively easy for schooling to become little more than children doing what teachers want them to do for them.

Even though school children may not always appreciate this significant fact about learning—that they are working for themselves, at least the teachers should have the distinction clearly in mind. Getting a child to work for himself is indeed a difficult teaching procedure, for it asks first for the clearing of pupil purposes in relationship to teaching goals and eventually for the clearing away of nonessential obstructions as the learner moves ahead.

8. *We must not mistake conformity for learning.*

Classrooms in our schools usually average about 35 children per teacher. The mere presence of this many children in one group situation acts as a pressure to push a teacher into uniform procedures and assignments.

Be it fourth grade, seventh, or tenth, ease of operation suggests first the same assignment for all, the same ground to be covered, with compromises where necessary. Pupil conformity to a given set of classroom conditions, common to all in the room, slips into the teacher's kit of tricks before she realizes it. And it is assumed that those who conform best to this given procedure learn best. The satisfaction the teacher receives from a child who willingly follows her directions may mislead her into concluding that learning is there.

The child's conformity to a prescribed classroom program is no assurance of learning. He may go through the day-by-day routine of meeting in all or in part the teacher's requirements, but growth is not necessarily assured. Learning is much more intricate than following directions, and teaching is much more intricate than giving them. Conformity will always have its rightful place in a classroom, but conformity alone must not be taken as assurance of learning.

9. *Learning begins where the learner is, not where the teacher is.*

In earlier days, as teachers we stood on the mountain top and tried to coax our students in the valley below to scale the heights and join us among the beauties above. Some reached us; many more gave up, discouraged. *Example:* In tenth year English we require Julius Caesar of all, regardless of level of reading ability or literary appreciation.

Today we begin with the student, determining first

GEE, KIDS, LOOK WHERE
TEACHER IS —

YOO-HOO,
CHILDREN,
HERE I AM
UP HERE

where he stands in respect to the particular area in which
we are working; then using all the teaching ingenuity
that we can muster, we begin the long and tedious climb
up the trail with him, going just as far as he can go. Some
will go to the mountain top: they may have been near it
to begin with; but others will climb but a short distance
this time. *Example:* We approach American literature by
determining what American literature is now functioning
in the lives of Tom, Dick, and Mary. If Tom is on the
Superman level; Dick, the Lone Ranger level; and Mary,
on the Book-of-the-Month Club level, our methods should
appreciate the fact.

If it is in establishing number concepts at fourth grade,
ability to write at second, or music appreciation at elev-
enth, the truth still holds. Only by knowing in so far as

possible the level at which your students now stand can you expect them to climb effectively with you toward higher goals. Growth always begins where the individual learner is, not where the teacher is. Get your teaching satisfactions from the progress he makes from that point and avoid the frustrations of his failure to reach a goal that you might arbitrarily set closer to yourself than to him. This simple principle of schooling denies no teacher the right to his teaching standards and ideals, but it asks that they be attuned to the realities at hand.

10. *Learning begins where the child is now, not where he was yesterday or where he will be tomorrow.*

Just as learning begins where the child is, not where the teacher is, so it begins where the child is now, not where he was yesterday or will be tomorrow.

To begin where he was some time ago lacks the stimulation of work geared to his present ability. To begin where he will be some time hence means discouragement, frustration, or disinterest.

To begin where the child is implies that the teacher knows him well, knows him in all the various ramifications of the fifth grade or whatever grade she is teaching. It means that she knows each child that way.

This necessity of close personal relationship between teacher and student invites the school to follow the plan of moving the teacher up with a class for two or three years. For instance, kindergarten, first, and second grade as a teaching sequence for a teacher before she goes back to pick up another kindergarten group. Third, fourth, and fifth, or fourth, fifth, and sixth are possibilities.

Some Pro's and Con's of Teaching

11. *The teacher cheats the child of part of his education unless he permits him to engage in all three of the closely related aspects of a learning situation, namely, (1) planning the experience, (2) carrying it out, and (3) evaluating it.*

In the traditional assign-study-recite pattern of schooling the pupil is permitted to engage in only the second of the three related aspects of a learning situation—carrying out the task. The teacher has done all the planning and has made the assignment. In this system, once the pupil has carried out the assignment the teacher alone will judge or grade the work.

In much of the classroom program teachers are finding it possible, and much more profitable educationally, to incorporate the pupil in the learning act from the very beginning and to include him in it to the very end. The pupil shares in planning the activities to be carried out, he carries them through, and when the work is brought to a conclusion he helps to evaluate his accomplishment. School days and school years are too short for teachers to cheat their pupils of valuable aspects of the learning situations.

12. *Growth in school cannot always be measured by a semester or even by a year.*

The graded system of American schools and the frequently accompanying mid-year entrance and promotion system have falsely encouraged teachers to think that growth can be measured by the semester or the year.

For a particular child, advancement in a formal school activity such as reading or writing or in a less formal one such as co-operating with the group may not be very noticeable in the course of one semester or one year. Such development comes in spurts and is not a steady thing. The typical marking and promotion system has led schools to judge pupil progress as though development were a steady process.

There is a growing tendency for teachers and schools to judge development in larger blocks of time. For instance, primary grades up through third might act as the first block. The teachers in that division get their satisfactions from seeing the difference in the development of the child between the time he enters the kindergarten and the time he leaves third grade, rather than on the basis of how much he advances in the five months of one semester.

The fourth, fifth, and sixth grades could be looked upon as another block for judging development. The seventh, eighth, and ninth grades could be grouped as a third block, and the three senior high years as another.

13. *The child has the right to receive the satisfactions of his schooling here and now, rather than to be promised delivery in the future.*

Every year there are schools all over America violating this simple psychological directive; they operate as though the main function of the work of each grade is to get the student into the next, as though the main purpose of attending elementary school is to pass on into that promised land—the high school. Once there, he finds:

> each lesson pointed toward the examination ahead,
> each examination pointed toward passing the course,
> each course pointed toward the credits to be received for it,
> each credit pointed toward graduation, and
> graduation pointed toward college or "life."

Subjects once passed have served their purpose in such a drive for the promised land, a conception of education that demands of the school no immediate satisfactions for the learner.

As a powerful lubricant for this pedagogical machinery, the marking system has been blended with grade promotion and the Carnegie unit-and-credit scheme. The threat of low marks and failure is used to keep the eyes of the weak and weary upon the step ahead, and the satisfaction

of high marks and honors serves as the come-on for the more competent.

The school needs to challenge to the utmost the abilities and talents of children, but the challenge needs to be made with emphasis upon intrinsic satisfactions in accomplishment and with due recognition of individual differences. There is competition in life, and there will always be the recognition of initiative in getting ahead in the world, but such competition outside the classroom usually recognizes capacities and limitations. The grocer does not compete with the plasterer; they have mutual respect for the abilities of the other. The man who appreciates the music of Beethoven does not see himself in competition with the one who likes only the currently popular dance bands. The woman who writes nothing more than an occasional letter to some member of her family does not compete in written composition with one who writes a daily column for the newspaper syndicate. The banker uses mathematics frequently, but in doing so he is not more honored than the physician who seldom uses it and then perhaps poorly.

Satisfactions in school accomplishment will be very meager for many children if these continue to be in the form of marks and honors, received as compensation for work past and as leads to better things still ahead.

14. *Use strengthens and disuse weakens.*

The eternal challenge to the schools will continue to be that of teaching those things that people find useful.

Although it took research studies to show the rate that information and skills once learned slip away when no longer called to use, the most common garden variety of teacher knows that her students are going to remember longest the things they will use and to forget soonest those that they won't use.

This is significant to a teacher in determining emphasis. For instance, the fourth-grade teacher who is teaching California as the social studies topic for the year will first determine the larger appreciations, attitudes, and understandings that she wishes to establish. She will then marshall the facts that will best help to establish these, realizing that the facts in themselves are likely to fall away from the learner in time, but that the larger appreciations, attitudes, and understandings are most likely to find continued use through subsequent life situations. And through such continued use they will be rounded out and strengthened.

Skill subjects, such as typing, are taught in the late high-school years, near the time those skills will be continued in the after-school office position. The skill of writing is taught in the early grades because the ability will be strengthened by the repeated use that will come in the following school grades. The teaching of spelling as lists of words unrelated to the child's everyday in-and-out-of-school use of words is an oversight of the fact that use of things once learned strengthens them and disuse weakens them.

15. *Praise is a greater educational force than blame.*

People do their best work when they are encouraged in their efforts. This is as true of children's work in the school as it is of mother's work in the home or dad's work at the office.

In the case of a child at any grade level, from kindergarten to twelfth grade, emphasis upon the little thing that he does well will pay far more educational dividends than criticism of the many things that he may be doing wrong.

Naturally, good teachers do not give false praise. Good teachers watch for the things they can commend, patiently encouraging the child to do the best that he can. Certainly there are wrong answers in the subtraction problems, but they will not be emphasized over and beyond the many more correct answers. There are still some teachers who wield a wicked red pencil, who make three misspelled words on a one-page book report seem more significant than the 150 correct ones.

It is the worth in the child's effort, feeble as it may be, that the good teacher is on the lookout for. There will be mistakes, but human nature seems to be set up in such a way that people advance on their accomplishments, not on their failures.

In addition to bringing better educational results, building students up through encouragement makes teaching a much more pleasant job than tearing them down through criticism. There are a number of research studies that have revealed that praise brings better educational results than blame.

16. *Educators need to respect the research that has been carried out in their profession, just as any other profession follows its findings.*

The teaching of reading in the lower grades, as practiced in most classrooms today, shows that we respect the research of this century in that area of instruction. However, at higher grade levels in instruction dealing with the use of the native language it is revealed that teachers rather generally ignore the findings of research.

For instance, research has shown that during the high school years a pupil's ability to pick out wrong verb forms in a grammar workbook may be doubled, but at the same time his actual use of verb forms in his everyday activities may not have improved noticeably. Furthermore, his use of language on the playground and in other social situations has improved practically none during these years of technical language study. Yet high-school English programs continue to be built around the formal study of word forms, sentence structure, and the related technicalities of grammar study.

There is no research to show that the most promising way to improve one's written or oral expression is through the continued study of formal grammar, yet the secondary school holds to the practice and permits the public to think it a false step to minimize this emphasis.

A teacher who is a true professional worker needs to be aware of the studies that have been conducted scientifically in his area of instruction, to know the findings, and to practice his calling in accordance with those findings.

Sometimes it is difficult for the layman to appreciate that ours is a profession that is backed by a body of research and experimentation just as is medicine or dentistry. But until educators themselves show such respect, it is hardly likely that laymen will do so.

Topics for Study and Discussion

1. Cite instances of instructional methods in which it would seem (1) that the teacher is trying *to give* learning to a child, and (2) that the teacher is trying *to promote* it with him.

2. What legislative action has been taken in this state concerning instruction in the field of citizenship?

3. If the principle is sound that "a student is working for himself rather than for the teacher," what techniques can a teacher of a particular subject use in applying this principle?

4. If the teacher wishes to begin instruction on the pupil's level what precautions can be taken in classroom procedure to effect this ideal?

5. In which of these three schools, elementary, secondary, and college, is the teacher more likely to permit the student to engage in all three of the aspects of a learning situation, as treated in principle 11? Account for this.

6. Where would the student of education find the best sources of information about educational research?

Chapter 6

The Teacher's Classroom

1. *It is in the classroom that most of the teacher's influence is exerted upon the pupil.*

This is not to minimize the educational values of the playground, the club, the field trip, the assembly, the library, and all of the other miscellaneous points of pupil-teacher contact. Rather, it is merely to give honor where honor is due.

Student teachers as well as leaders of education continue to search for the common denominators of good classrooms. For in so doing they hope to establish the basic formula that will enable the student of education to say, "These are the things that make up the successful classroom." Unfortunately, the creation of the good classroom cannot be simplified into law or precept.

It would be extremely difficult for any group of either experienced or inexperienced teachers to agree upon a list of *things never to do in the classroom* and a list of *things always to do in a classroom.* Invariably there is injected in the list such conditioning words and phrases as *maybe—at times—usually—under most circumstances—*and *when possible.*

This reflects the strong position that the teacher holds in the educational scheme of things. It reflects the wide variation among human talents, among teaching personalities, and consequently among good classroom approaches. In advancing this short chapter, the writer appreciates the fact that whole courses are offered in the study of classroom methods and techniques. The attempt here is to set down a few principles of classroom operation that come close to that common denominator of good classrooms that teachers will continue to seek.

2. *Kindness is the first quality of a good teacher.*

There has never been agreement about the qualities of the good teacher, for our schools are full of good teachers and no two of them are alike. However, it can be safely said that the one quality that they have in common is kindness. Among those who have not attained the stature worthy of the title *good teacher* are those who must shout at children, those who are irritated by the natural behavior of children, those who can't operate a classroom without using their physical force on children, and those who can never warm up to a few individuals in the class.

Regardless of how great the shortage of teachers ever becomes, there is no place in the American classroom for the man or woman who in either thought or action is not kind to boys and girls. Better to close a classroom than to subject children to an unkind teacher under the guise of education.

There was a time in the history of schools when the educational theorist was afraid of the warm hearted teacher, afraid lest he not exert the severity that would bring the results expected. To be kind to children does not mean to sacrifice one's instructional ideals, any more than to be unreasonably severe with children means to accomplish high instructional aims.

DIRECTING THE LEARNING SITUATION

3. The teacher is a director of learning rather than a hearer of lessons.

School teaching once followed the simple formula of assign-study-recite. Each day the teacher made the assignment for tomorrow's lesson, the pupil studied the lesson at home that night, and come the dawn he recited it back as questions were directed to the class. And then a new assignment, more outside study, another recitation, and so on and on through the school term.

The bulk of the class period was given over to the recitation, in which the teacher attempted to determine the amount of learning that had taken place, the extent to which the pupils had mastered the material or covered the ground assigned the previous day. Pupils recited for the teacher and were marked accordingly.

But unfortunately for schools and school teachers, learning is not as simple as that. In the modern school the teacher's role is one of far greater significance than that of hearer of lessons. It is one that enables him to share to the fullest extent with his pupils his greater experience and maturity. Of course there are lessons to hear but there is much more besides.

If he assumes the greater position of director of learning, he must first have a fair idea of how learning takes place. He must determine where the learning is to lead those who happen to be in the class. He must sense the returns his teaching contribution is making to our country's investment in education for democracy. He must know the possibilities, the potentialities of each student. He must see this work in relationship to the total life of each. He must take time to plan with other teachers and supervisors the whole learning situation of the school. He must do all this and even more if he is to qualify as a director of learning. Those teachers who cannot make the grade will slip back and continue as hearers of lessons.

4. *A teacher should always give the child the benefit of the doubt.*

My first superintendent, J. O. Chewning, was always passing on to his beginning teachers some of the homespun Hoosier philosophy that he brought up to his office with him from his early days on the Ohio River. He anticipated

that a beginning teacher at times was bound to have his misgivings about the human race and especially that portion of it that was in his classroom. He anticipated that a beginning teacher at times might even be inclined to suspect some of the pupils of having instigated or perpetrated classroom disturbances, to suspect them merely because of their previous difficulties.

John O. Chewning also knew that a teacher, especially a beginner, was at times going to wonder how he should mark a pupil at the end of a grading period or at the end of a semester.

His advice in this whole realm of teacher-pupil relationships was, "When in doubt, give the benefit of the doubt to the pupil."

RELATIONSHIPS WITH CHILDREN

5. *The teacher does not have a dual role to play.*

Our professional libraries are full of studies that have

been made to determine what children want their teachers to be like, and they all come out with approximately what we might expect. They can be summarized with the statement that the qualities we want in our respected friends and companions in everyday life situations are wanted in the classrooms by the students.

A sad commentary on the profession is that ever so often there appears in a high-school newspaper a student's story under some such headline as, "Teachers Are Human After All." The fact that too often such a thing has to be discovered or that it is announced as news for others to know about is a reflection on something or other in the teaching set-up. If we as teachers are inclined to assume a second role of life as we step into the schoolhouse, is it because tradition has passed down a schoolroom environment that overpowers us, or is it because we harbor in our minds a prudish conception of the classroom role that tends to make us play a fictitious part while there?

Let's first be ourselves, at all times and in all places, and then let the teacher role take care of itself. Naturally, the fine character and good judgment that are asked of the one who succeeds in the teaching profession will enable the teacher to be himself at all times. The teaching position can never be acted as a stage role to be assumed only on special occasions.

6. *Every teacher should take time to become well acquainted with a new class of students before making any major assignments.*

Eight pages of history or fifteen problems in applied arithmetic have no place as an assignment for the first or second day of the school other than to enable the teacher to know better how he can serve the various pupils.

When the writer once suggested to a staff of high-school teachers that they withhold assignments for a few days of warming up exercises, it was surprising how helpless or lost a few of them were when deprived of their subject matter for even two or three days. This brings up the suggestion that the good teacher is the one who has much more in common with his students than merely the subject matter.

The leisurely, yet businesslike approach of the kindergarten teacher the first week of school has something in the way of a lesson for elementary, high school, and even college teachers. There is no specific subject matter to be hurried into, no books that have to be read, in fact no books that can be read. Consequently, she sets about the task of becoming acquainted with the children and helping them to settle down to an adjustment that in time will bring the desired educational results.

We have all seen the teacher who was so busy getting into the work the first day, it was late in the term before he discovered that he didn't really know some of the pupils.

PLANS, CONTESTS, AND TECHNIQUES

7. *Regardless of how long he has served the profession, no teacher should enter a classroom without a lesson plan developed for that specific class.*

A teacher may have three classes of English 7, but each calls for its unique lesson plan. The difference in the classes is represented in the three unique groups of pupils. Only when the subject, and not the child, is the teacher's main concern can one lesson plan serve the three classes of English 7.

A fourth-grade teacher may have the same group of children all day, five days a week, but each day calls for a well conceived lesson plan. There may be a unit of work underway that will continue for two or three weeks, but some re-planning has to be done for each day in the light of the successes and failures of the day before.

A teacher may teach a subject such as chemistry for 25 years, but each year calls for new planning. Any subject takes on new meaning each year from (1) the new group of pupils to be served by it and (2) the constantly changing social setting of which the school and all of its work are a part.

Lesson planning begins with goals of instruction for the time-period in question and ends with a well conceived means of arriving at those goals.

8. *Classroom procedure should not resemble a contest in which the teacher is pitted against the student.*

From time to time there have crept into the classroom certain teaching procedures that would leave the impression that, somewhere along the line, we were encouraged to look at the classroom as a contest between teacher and student, a contest justifying a bit of deception on either side if the teacher or pupil could get by with it. A few traces of this conception of schooling are these:

1. Teachers' questions are used regularly for the purpose of catching students who have not done their home work. The daily recitation of numerous short questions is used to catch idlers as much as it is used to develop concepts from facts.

2. A student notes carefully the order in which the teacher goes up and down the classroom rows with her questions, in order to gird himself ahead of time for the specific points that may be asked when she gets to him.

3. In this question-answer contest, the student often has his book open before him and steals a look now and then in anticipation of the question about to come.

4. "Beating around the bush" in giving his answer is commonly resorted to by the student who doesn't know the answer to the question asked him, but who wants to retain his position in the teacher's scheme of things.

5. In following the assign-study-recite classroom procedure, the teacher often keeps grade book in hand, rating each effort or lack of effort in contest style.

6. In especially the objective type of teacher's examination, it is not uncommon to find a trick question or two included, in an attempt to catch a student in his thinking.

7. Evaluating pupil progress, which is done at the end of a grading period, is a right retained by the teacher rather than a right shared with the pupils, again pitting the pupil against teacher. Complaints about unfair marks are made by the bolder members of the class.

8. In preparing papers and notebooks outside of class, pupils use the work of classmates freely, feeling that a bit of deception is fair as long as the teacher doesn't detect it.

This teacher-pupil contest conception of schooling has grown up most frequently in the classrooms and at the grade levels where the coverage of subject matter, the assign-study-recite method of teaching, and the marking system are all three over emphasized.

The classroom is not an arena for jousting between teacher and pupil. It is headquarters for a co-operative program of work emphasizing meaningful activities of the pupils, the teacher being there to encourage and lead the pupils in such activities.

Teachers are not there to catch students. Students are not there to deceive teachers. Instructional methods that encourage this are questionable.

9. *Techniques of teaching should be the slaves of teachers rather than teachers being the slaves of techniques.*

As teachers we must constantly force ourselves to question why we do this and that, for only by doing so can we keep in mind the worthy goals of instruction which, after all, are the justification of our teaching methods.

Why do I use a progress chart in writing posted in the corner of my room? It is nothing sacred in itself. I once adopted it to help me encourage children along the road to better writing. Does it help? Maybe I have used it so long that I have forgotten that it was merely a technique that I tried.

Why do I use these after-school detention slips? It is punishment to the child, but is punishment my teaching goal? No, my goals are such things as developing language facility, learning to work co-operatively on a common problem, understanding America better, and so on. The after-school detention period is a technique that I once picked up along the way. Does it help me to reach these instructional goals? If it doesn't, maybe I'd better try something else.

Order and Discipline

10. *The type of order needed in a classroom is in direct relationship to the nature of the work to be done at the moment.*

Classroom order is not something to be worked for independently of the studies and the activities to be carried on in the room. The teacher who worries about classroom control in itself is apt to make the matter an obsession that may supersede the real purpose of the classroom situation.

The eagerness and curiosity expressed by primary children, leading on into finding-out and sharing their discoveries with others, suggest a businesslike atmosphere in a room that should have the right of way over classroom order for its own sake.

Fifth-graders who are engaged intensively at some reference work, each on his own, demand a quiet classroom in which they can concentrate. The disturbance made by one is unfair to the others.

Under the direction of a discriminating teacher, a classroom of pupils come to sense the distinctions among the different types of work situations that come during a day or a week and to adjust accordingly. The atmosphere will range from almost complete silence to a businesslike hustle-and-bustle that always resembles confusion.

11. *Discipline is something more than good classroom order.*

Discipline as such took the center of the stage in the old school. This was natural, for it was so often a take-it-or-leave-it school, with little concern for the pupil as an

individual and, consequently, little compromise between teacher-demand and pupil-ability. The curriculum was a preordained affair considered good for all, and that was that. Naturally, disciplinary problems were many, and the control of students was a popular topic at educational gatherings.

Even today the dictionary passes down this early conception of discipline as a classroom-order, with this definition of the word: "Order as maintained in a military organization, prison, or schoolroom." Today in the profession we speak little of discipline. The fine spirit that exists in our schools between children and teachers reflects the continuous development of teacher training and the increased understanding of our job. The teacher feels an obligation to and appreciation of individual worth, and consequently curriculum adjustment to needs and interests is in greater esteem than are the uniform molds into which children were once forced by teacher command. There is so much meaningful work going on in the modern classroom that the center of attention is upon such activity rather than upon keeping order. Order comes naturally.

The teacher does not take advantage of his position as the one with the authority, the one who can threaten, the one privileged to use sarcasm, in short, the one who can push others around. He assures himself of control so that learning activities can go forward, but in doing so he takes advantage of a group situation that promises maximum development. The greater the time and attention that a teacher gives to planning a rich program of instruction, the less the time and attention that he must give to classroom order.

12. *Good discipline is self-discipline.*

Today, just as yesterday, the teacher is concerned about discipline, but this concern is educational, not pedagogical. That is, he sees self-discipline as a basis of successful group living in America, and he uses every opportunity to give the students a chance to develop their abilities to control themselves—to manage their own affairs. The spirit that he wishes in his group is the spirit that marks misdemeanor as trespass upon the group's rights, rather than as misdemeanor against the teacher as one in command. He strives for a natural work situation that will not collapse when he leaves the room.

If he is teaching in a high school rather than in an elementary school, and is assigned a study hall, he should be concerned about the obligation to teach American youth to handle themselves. To sit at the front of a study hall on guard is perhaps easier than educating the group to self-direction. Teachers sitting in study halls are dead giveaways of the failure of classroom instruction in citizenship.

Children and youth do not learn self-discipline through speeches, correct classroom answers, and editorials, but through practice in control, which follows knowledge. It is easy for us to drive within the speed limit if a police car is cruising behind; in study hall it is easy for children to work if the teacher is cruising among the rows of seats.

GOOD DISCIPLINE IS SELF-DISCIPLINE

Democracy is understood only as it is lived, and it cannot be lived in schools unless teachers carefully provide the situations for living it. Good discipline is self-discipline, whether in school or in life in general. Into a good teaching situation goes teaching ideals, knowledge, pupil desire, and then practice.

13. *In the classroom, just as in the larger unit of American democracy, there can be no freedom without responsibility.*

A democratic society does not award the individual the freedom for which it stands, but rather, it gives him the chance to achieve his freedom through proper social action. And so it is in the schoolroom. A teacher operating a democratic classroom does not award the pupil freedom, but rather enables him to achieve his freedom through proper social action. The individual in either situation exchanges responsibility for freedom.

In the lower grade rooms the child feels the freedom of moving about the room, going to and from the book tables, the easels, and the work benches. But in the process of achieving this he has learned that in return he has assumed responsibility for proper behavior.

The expectancy of proper behavior, which was at first centered mainly in the teacher, in time becomes a group-expectancy, in which the children as a class expect each member to show this responsibility for personal action.

The room in which the teacher gives freedom without expecting anything in return becomes a room in which anarchy rather than democracy reigns. Such conditions are satisfying to neither child nor teacher.

The school in which the right to freedom is not extended by the faculty, in which children always march to teacher order, is a school that cheats the American public in the investment it is making in education for citizenship.

Since democratic action is not inherited but must be learned, the teacher must work diligently to set up situations in which children can practice the ways of democracy. Although the rights to freedom in a group of children are equal at the outset, all the children may not achieve their freedoms at the same time or in the same degree. The freedom-respecting teacher lets each walk alone just as soon as possible and just as far as possible. Society always has difficulty in getting some to control their own movements. So it may be in a classroom.

It is not the teacher's place to wait until children want freedoms. It is his obligation to create the desire and to help them learn to assume the corresponding responsibilities.

14. *Application in the classroom cannot be taken at face value as learning.*

The typical classroom situation of 35 or 40 pupils has invited, or at times even driven, teachers to adopt practices and materials that represent little more than busy work for the class members. Among such practices are these:

In a history class the teacher has the children recite from the book, taking turns reading the topic sentence in bold type and explaining what was said in that paragraph or section.

In language study all the pupils, regardless of ability and needs, do the same exercises in a formal grammar workbook.

While she is teaching reading to one third of the class in the front of the room, the teacher has the other first-grade children color uniform outline drawings that she has prepared and passed out to them.

In an algebra class, while he is helping a few pupils who do not understand the equations being studied, the teacher keeps the faster students busy at their desks working more examples of the equations that they have already shown that they understand well.

Application is essential to learning, but the good teacher knows that mere application in itself is not necessarily learning. The good teacher distinguishes sharply between learning activities and busy work.

Judging Pupil Progress

15. *It is relatively easy to misuse the marking system.*

Marks, often called grades, should hardly be used as threats for failure to work or as promises for good work done. They represent extrinsic values, and the wise teacher wants her students to work for the satisfactions that are in the learning experiences themselves.

If you direct a class with grade-book in hand, mechanically checking the fate of each after his recitation, you run the risk of injecting a performance-for-teacher atmosphere into the classroom. The total, or the average, of all these little marks in a book is, after all, a rather cold or artificial indication of the development that has taken place with a child who has been under your influence for a month, a semester, or a year.

The teacher can very well use the marking system as a means by which students can help check their progress from time to time. If the pupil has purposes of his own and spends a period of time trying to get to the goals those purposes represent, then certainly he and the teacher might well determine together his accomplishment or his progress at that particular moment. This is quite differ-

ent from leaving the marks in the hands of the teacher to be handed out as pay for services rendered.

If marks become the chief incentive for work in a school and if keen competition is encouraged for these rewards, the school must be prepared to cope with copying, cribbing, and similar underhand methods that are the shady companions of the system. Students who work for themselves rather than for teacher or extrinsic reward, take high marks and teacher commendation in stride.

If you open the year's work with your class by outlining what is necessary to pass to the next grade or to get the two credits offered, you are not only emphasizing false values, but you are placing yourself in a position of having to fail students who do not reach the minimum requirements that you've set up. You would be outlining all the requirements and expectations before you have had time to know your students, their capabilities, interests, and needs. In short, you'd be violating that other principle of teaching: the student is more important than the subject. We must continue to seek reporting systems that do not hinder us from respecting individual worth in whatever kind of package it comes to us.

16. *Tests test the teacher as much as they test the student.*

In the upper years of the elementary school and in the high school, the giving of teacher-made tests is common procedure all over America. In form they range from the test of five or six essay questions on over to the true-false test of a hundred short statements.

In almost every school there is the teacher who is shocked at the low marks that his pupils make on his monthly test, the teacher who casts the blame upon the class and lets the matter go at that.

Likewise in every school there is the teacher who is challenged by the low marks that his pupils make on his test, challenged to study the disaster to determine where the error lies. Didn't he teach them these things? Is it a reflection upon his teaching?

Or was there something wrong with his test? Maybe the questions were too difficult. Maybe the wording was obscure. Maybe the questions were misleading in some instances. Maybe the class was not at ease in taking the test. Maybe they were misled as to the ground to be covered. Maybe his scoring of the essay answers was too severe. Maybe he needed to study more carefully the art of testing.

Test-making is a difficult task, calling for careful study and planning on the part of the teacher. Unless properly designed, tests will never bring to teachers the satisfactions that they deserve from their teaching efforts.

17. *Teachers need to be actively engaged in community enterprises touching the typical affairs and problems of their community.*

The teacher who commutes to his work, who does not live in the school community, is handicapped in making a maximum contribution to the work of the school. Any public school gets its being from its supporting community. There, in that community, are the will to support the school and the points of view of schooling with which the school staff must be fully acquainted. There, in that community, are the children to be served, as well as their out-of-school activities into which the school must correlate its program.

Close home-school relationships, which are so essential to a good school program, are best furthered by a staff of teachers who in common with the parents feel that particular community as home.

The teacher needs to be a participant in community endeavors, a citizen known by a fair percentage of the fellow townspeople for these civic contributions over and beyond the service to the school proper. The teacher who knows the community through active participation is more apt to bring into the classroom that balance of realism that is so essential. The teacher's classroom reflects his relationship to the school community.

TOPICS FOR STUDY AND DISCUSSION

1. Attempt to establish a list of *things to do* in the classroom and a list of *things not to do* in the classroom, keeping in mind general application to schools all over the nation. In the discussion, recognize the influence of factors such as grade level and subject.

2. Does a beginning teacher need to spend any time planning a definite course of action to assure being liked by the pupils?

3. Special emphasis is placed upon lesson planning in this chapter. What are the general features of good lesson plans?

4. Describe the procedures used in a classroom that you have observed, in which there was no semblance of a teacher-student contest.

5. Of the seventeen principles set out in this chapter, choose one that seems to contradict commonly accepted educational theory and practice. Point out the discrepancies.

6. In what ways can a teacher place responsibilities upon pupils in the classroom in keeping with their maturity? Refer to specific grade levels and subject field.

7. Does principle 14 apply to any one of these levels more than the others, elementary, secondary, and college?

Chapter **7**

The Pupil's Place in the School

1. *The pupil has status of two distinct types in the school: his legal status and his social status.*

The right of a child to attend school may or may not bear direct relationship to his ultimate position in the school or in a teacher's classroom. The law assures him certain legal status in respect to school membership and attendance. However, once he is there, it remains for the administrator and the teacher to help him secure the social status that is necessary if he is to succeed, social status meaning a proper position in his teacher's as well as in his classmates' scheme of things. This calls for true understanding of pupils.

This chapter is presented on the supposition that it is just as urgent to outline the road to social status in the school as it is to review the state statutes that define the legal status of the pupil. In entering teaching we first become acquainted with the things to be taught, and as time goes on we become more fully acquainted with the children to be taught.

2. *There's a lot to be learned about children from books and courses, but there's a lot more to be learned from the children themselves.*

137

Although a full understanding of children is dependent upon experience, the beginning teacher has at hand sound principles that aid in the classroom approach. In the pages that follow are presented first, the pupil's legal status and

second, a set of principles that may help us discover his desirable social position in the classroom.

The Pupil's Legal Status

3. *The child's school attendance represents a combination of a privilege, a right, and an obligation.*

As demonstrated in Chapter 2, a state is obligated by its constitution to establish and maintain a system of free public schools. In turn, the state offers the children within its confines the privilege of free attendance in these schools, this right being regulated by specifications dealing with such matters as age and residence. But the state is not satisfied to recognize the child's right and to extend to him the privilege to attend school. It sets compulsory attendance ages and places a statutory obligation upon parents to send their children to school in accordance with this law. The preparation for citizenship that is so vital to the welfare of the American nation cannot leave schooling as merely the right or the privilege of the child.

4. *In schooling, as in other aspects of American citizenship, with the rights and privileges go also obligations and responsibilities.*

Compulsory School Attendance. Most of the states, 32 of them, set 7 to 16 as the age range for compulsory school attendance.[1] These states are:

Alabama, Arkansas, Connecticut, Delaware, Florida, Georgia, Idaho, Illinois, Indiana, Iowa, Kansas, Kentucky, Louisiana, Maryland, Massachusetts, Mississippi, Missouri, Nebraska, New Jersey, New York, North Carolina, Oregon, Rhode Island, South Carolina, South Dakota, Tennessee, Texas, Vermont, Virginia, West Virginia, Wisconsin, and Wyoming.

Also requiring part-time school attendance up to age 18 are these states of the above group: Illinois, Indiana, Louisiana (for girls only), Missouri, and Oregon.

Seven states set 8 to 16 as the compulsory attendance age requirements: Arizona, California, Colorado, Minnesota, Montana, New Hampshire, and Washington. In this group California requires part-time attendance up to age 18.

The other states follow these general regulations: 6-16,

---

[1] Statistics reported here from the United States Office of Education, 1950.

Michigan; 6-17, New Mexico; 6-18, Ohio; 7-17, Maine and North Dakota; 7-18, Nevada and Oklahoma; 8-17, Pennsylvania; and 8-18, Utah.

Naturally, there are many minor stipulations in these school laws that make actual comparison more difficult than the general groupings above would indicate. In the main, the variations treat the exemptions from compulsory attendance. Again, generalizing, the exemptions are more commonly based on (1) the need for employment, (2) physical or mental disability, (3) attendance at private school or private instruction, and (4) distance from school or lack of transportation.

All state regulations are supplemented by those of the local school districts, but in case of conflict the state authority is upheld. For instance, the National Education Association calls attention to two interesting school attendance cases in Mississippi and Louisiana dealing with marriage.[2]

Mississippi Case. A Mississippi schoolboard denied admission to a child of school age because of the fact that she had married, on the grounds that the admission of married children would be detrimental to the good government and usefulness of the schools. Later the court ruled:

> . . . it is commendable in married persons of school age to desire to further pursue their education, and thereby become better fitted for the duties of life. And they are as much subject to the rules of the school as unmarried pupils, and punishable to the same extent for a breach of such rules.

[2] As reported in *The Legal Status of the Public-School Pupil,* N.E.A. Research Bulletin, Vol. 26 No. 1, February, 1948, pp. 6, 15.

Louisiana Case. In this state, a court case of recent years relieves from school attendance a married person still of compulsory school age, on the grounds that marriage "imposes obligations upon the parties that are obviously inconsistent with compulsory school attendance."

Maximum School Age. The maximum free school age in 29 states is age 21.[3] The exceptions are:

> Age 20: Missouri, New Jersey, Virginia, and Wisconsin.
> Age 18: Louisiana, Nevada, New Mexico, Utah, and Vermont.
> No maximum: California, Connecticut, Florida, Georgia, Indiana, Massachusetts, Michigan, New Hampshire, Rhode Island, and Tennessee.

And so, the great majority of the states by legislation assure a child at least fifteen or sixteen years of free schooling. There is every indication in this democratic gesture that the American intention is for individual teachers to do their utmost to respect this right. The teacher's respect for individual pupils comes through two main avenues: (1) the acceptance of him as a worthy member of the class and (2) the presentation of a classroom program suited to his unique nature. It is not always easy for a teacher to show wholehearted acceptance of the child who seems not to want to avail himself of the privilege to attend school.

5. *In the case of unjustified absence or tardiness of a school child, the teacher should hesitate before placing the blame on the child.*

Just because the child is more accessible than the par-

---

3 *The Legal Status of the Public-School Pupil,* p. 7.

ent is no reason that the school should place the blame for unjustified absence upon the child. Although a school district has the right to do so, in very few cases do schools go to court against a parent whose child continually violates the compulsory school attendance law. The inconvenience or difficulty of reaching the parent in such instances may invite school authorities and teachers to place the blame, pressure, and punishment only upon the child.

It is the parent who violates the compulsory attendance law, and not the child. The sympathy of an understanding teacher can go a long way toward mending the improper attendance habits of a child who can secure little help in such matters from other sources.

THE PUPIL'S SOCIAL STATUS

6. *Whether he realizes it or not, a feeling of belongingness is the first thing that a school child asks of the new classroom or the new school that he enters.*

In their movement through schools, children and youth are always entering new groups, are always more or less dependent upon new teachers to hold out a welcoming hand to them. Where promotions are made on a semester basis, it is not unusual for the primary or middle grade child to be changed from one group to another at the middle of the school year. The pressure of numbers and the ever-present problem of pupil-teacher ratio account for this.

A new room, a new teacher-face, a new social group, can be mighty strange things to a lower grade child, even though he has been attending the school for two or three years. The desire to be accepted, to belong, is not a fancy; it is an imperative thing. At high-school level it reaches such a state of significance that the nature of the adjustment often means the difference between staying in school or quitting.

School life is a life of group situations. The child wants to be respected by his group, his mates, and his teacher. In high school, such satisfactions come readily to those who make good marks and to those who make the teams

SPEARS

and the top billings in other activities. Others turn from school to a pay envelope, a uniform, an automobile, or even to unsocial actions to secure a feeling of importance.

The entrance-to-school of a child or youth, be he in the elementary school, the junior high, or the senior high, should upon the very day of entrance act as a challenge to the school to find the best possible adjustment for him in classroom, activity, and social setting. Once he has been permitted to fail or in any other way has been made to feel that he does not belong, the possibilities of maximum adjustment are lessened significantly.

7. One of the biggest challenges to a teacher is the true recognition of the worth of each pupil.

True democracy respects the worth of every individual, whatever his origin or present status. True democracy in the classroom respects the worth of every pupil, whatever his origin or his present status in the work of the room.

The child should not lose caste with the teacher just because he rates low in reading ability, number skill, or ability to write. Neither should he lose caste with the teacher just because he is not as skillful as his mates in following such democratic principles as cooperating with the group, respecting proper leadership, or assuming responsibility for his own actions.

The child who is handicapped in the common tools of learning deserves the sympathetic attention of the teacher, not her blame or disinterest. The child who is handicapped in assuming a helpful role in the classroom group situation is just as deserving of help as is the one who is elected best citizen by his group.

The teaching profession is well populated with teachers who place the worth of each individual child before all else. That minority group that cannot exalt individual worth above scholastic accomplishment find teaching an exceedingly tiresome task.

8. Faith in human nature is an essential to teaching.

There was once a printing teacher who suspected the worst of each new class. Boys had thrown type in his shop before, and he didn't wait for the newcomers to do so; he warned them all not to throw type the first period they were in his room.

There was a fourth-grade teacher who was preparing to make bean bags with her children. She warned them all not to poke beans up their noses.

There was a seventh-grade teacher who was giving a written test in arithmetic. After she had distributed the paper and before the questions had been placed on the board, she suggested to each child that he keep the paper covered with his arm to prevent his neighbors from seeing his work.

But—

There was a teacher who permitted her second graders to leave her room at recess without marching in front of her, because, as she told them, she knew that they were big enough to handle themselves quietly. Those who couldn't were aided by her to achieve the ability to do so.

And there was a high school that never used teachers in study halls because the faculty had a faith in the student body that paid educational dividends. The faculty helped the students to achieve the ability to control themselves.

It was more difficult to teach a group of children to handle themselves properly in leaving the room on their own than it was always to lead them. It was more difficult to bring high-school pupils to the desire and the ability to handle their own study halls than it was to sit over them every minute of the study-hall period. But likewise, it was more educational.

9. *No two pupils are alike.*

There is constant reference in educational literature to the differences in "needs, interests, and abilities" that exist among school children. If as a teacher you dedicate yourself to this elementary principle that no two pupils are alike, you take a heavy load upon your shoulders, but if psychologically honest you can take no other course. It is easier to say that pupils are different than to do something about it.

Intelligence quotients, reading scores, and similar measurements don't tell the whole story of differences, but they are enough to act as the handwriting on the wall for the teacher who would dare pass out uniform requirements for a class and hold to a common standard of attainment. A casual glance over the group before you should act as a similar warning.

Once they had discovered that children are different at any given grade level, educational technicians felt that we could master the problem of differences by ability grouping. After years of valiant trial, it is generally realized today that children do not lend themselves to such exact sorting. By trial and error, with emphasis upon the latter, school administrators have learned that there can be no true homogeneous grouping unless classes of one are set up. For just as soon as we place two pupils together, individual differences invite attention. The human being is a complex entity that defies the grading and sorting that is practiced in marketing lemons and retailing bath towels. Even the runt that is sorted out of the new litter of pigs may turn out to be quite a surprise to the farmer who did the grading.

There is still the opportunity for a teacher to group within a class, to show respect for differences. But today the wise teacher knows that no automatic system of grouping is going to perform wonders in itself.

After all the care that administrators, guidance workers, and parents have or have not taken in seeing that the right child gets into the right course or right class, the challenge of differences is still there for you to contend with as a teacher. Classrooms would be monotonous if it were not so. Intelligence quotients, reading scores, and other more or less mechanical readings are no substitute for close personal relationships, but they do help to unlock the doors to differentiated teaching materials and reasonable teaching expectations.

Understanding the Normal Child

10. *Teachers need to appreciate what a normal child is.*

Some teachers retain an idealistic conception of school pupils that is all out of line with the realities of the world. Take, for example, a group of normal thirteen-year-olds as they come out of a movie or off a public playground. They will range in shoe size from 3 to 12, in swimming ability from a rock to a fish, in sociability from minus-nothing to super salesmanship, in writing ability from mere legibility to Spencerian perfection, in reading speed and comprehension from fourth-grade level to twelfth-grade level.

We need to remind ourselves that the scores on standardized tests, such as the silent reading tests, are, after all, based on norms determined on the basis of a school organization of grades and school tasks, and that life outside the school does not conform to such norms. Even though a tenth-grader may have a reading ability at fifth-grade level, that ability may be normal for him and should be accepted as such by the teacher.

We need to fight the artificial concept of a normal student, which in itself implies sub-normals and above-normals. Here again, the concept springs from our ideas of the grades in an educational ladder. By and large, of every 200 boys and girls who enter a senior high school from a junior high or an elementary school, 200 of them are normal. They become sub-normals and above-normals in the thinking of teachers only if those teachers have rather fixed ideas of a tenth-grade curriculum in English, history, or what-not.

11. *Although no two pupils are alike, the vast majority can be classified as normal youngsters, and their differences need not be accentuated by the school.*

It is normal for some children to be noisier than others, some to be more active, some to be poorer readers, some to be less tidy, some to be less co-operative, some to be more dictatorial, and so on. Although good teachers will do all possible to appreciate shortages, strengths, and needs, and to serve each child to the fullest extent, in doing so they will not accentuate these natural differences among children.

Some years ago in this country, educators went to seed on trying to dissect any given class of children into innumerable homogeneous groups within the class. If a class entering a junior high school numbered 210, it was not uncommon to find an administrator meticulously grading them by intelligence quotient into seven ability groups, ranging down the scale from top 30 pupils to low 30.

In some schools there has been the tendency for a teacher to look upon any deviation from orthodox behavior as indication of a so-called problem child, subject for guidance counselor or psychologist.

The invitation to appreciate the differences among people, which our profession extends to each teacher, carries with it the warning that such differences are to be expected and that the segregation of individuals for special treatment is to be the exception rather than the rule. Once differences are appreciated as normal and to be expected, ability grouping takes on a wholesome atmosphere and loses any tinge of sorting the promising from the unpromising.

12. *It is necessary that the teacher understand children or youth as a group, in addition to understanding them as individuals.*

The primary teacher needs to know the general characteristics of children in the age range from 4 to 9 and the nature of growth and development at the primary age. Only then is she able to appreciate and to help the individual. The primary teacher has at her disposal today valuable information about the general characteristics of five-year olds, six-year olds, seven-year olds, and so on. Most fifth or sixth graders have something in common.

The high-school teacher needs to appreciate that distinct population group commonly referred to as youth. He should know the basic developmental needs of that age group, as well as recognize the place that their elders' society has or has not made for them in respect to the important things to be done in that society.

Any teacher of experience should know that there are at least four basic characteristics of youth who are going through the high school years: (1) the desire for independence, (2) the desire to be accepted, (3) the drive to achieve proper social relationships, and (4) the drive to secure a proper set of values to serve behavior. Many of the things that pupils do in and around the school reflect

these natural aspects of this growing-up period. Good work habits, proper achievement in school studies, and good school citizenship can all be emphasized by the wise teacher who sees their relationships to these basic characteristics of youth.

Growing up is no easy task. It is quite troublesome for the one doing the growing, even though teachers and parents would like to feel that the trouble is theirs rather than the child's.

13. *A teacher may learn more about a specific child in two or three conferences with the parent than in two or three courses in the graduate school.*

A great deal of emphasis has been and is still being given to the question of home reports, the cards that the school sends home periodically reporting on the progress of the child in school. Little if any emphasis has ever been given to a systematic reporting of the home to the school, and not enough attention has been given to the matter of soliciting and securing from the parent the information so pertinent to the school's full understanding of the child.

Perhaps the first home report should be just that—a systematic report that the home makes to the school at the time the child first enters. Certainly the parent's 24-hour-a-day contact with the child for the first five or six years of his life are not to be overlooked when the teacher is seeking an early understanding of her new class of first graders or kindergartners.

In recent years the educational profession has adopted as almost uniform procedure the accumulative school record card that is to be sent with the pupil from the school below, as he enters the school above. But it is indeed surprising that teachers in this school above have placed so much faith in this accumulation of professional opinion, without thinking of asking the parent for his or her suggestions about the entering pupil.

Not until at least one grading period has passed does the average teacher get around to consulting a parent of a pupil, and then such consultation often springs from a maladjustment already effected. The wise teacher is the one who works diligently to confer early with a maximum number of the parents of his new pupils. Two or three wholesome conferences with a parent are much more effective than a more prolonged study of children in general.

EAGERNESS AND SUCCESS

14. *Eagerness to do things is not restricted to the brighter children.*

The teacher's slow-learning group is just as eager to do things as is the fast-moving section of the class, if the teacher keeps the activities within their sphere of ability. It is when the activities provided are above the level of ability that the children seem dull.

Picture-method materials in aiding number readiness and in advancing simple science concepts help primary teachers keep alive the eagerness of all children. Differentiating the questions in the news period to serve varied abilities and interests whets eagerness.

At high-school level, the literature class that is built on differentiated readings, with ample use of such related aids as films and transcriptions, is more apt to assure eagerness on the part of a maximum number of students than is the class with the same classic required of all.

The teacher who may be inclined to feel that eagerness to do things is restricted to the brighter children should take advantage of the opportunities to mix with children in out-of-class situations. Eagerness, activity, and even ingenuity seem to find no intellectual barriers on the playground or in the social or recreational gathering.

15. *The ability to succeed in a course or in a piece of work within a course does not necessarily assure profit from the work.*

Detailed accumulative records, intelligence quotients, reading scores, and diagnostic and aptitude tests are used by the modern high school to help in determining the possible or probable success of the entering pupils in the different courses offered. For the child leaving the elementary school, it is usually a relatively simple matter to determine his ability to succeed in such a high-school course as algebra, history, or French.

However, teachers helping to guide pupils into courses at the next grade level must remember that the fact that a person succeeds in a course is no assurance that he profits by it. An example from mathematics will suffice.

High schools offer both algebra and an applied arithmetic course in the ninth year. It is common for the schools to direct into the algebra course those pupils who have been most successful in elementary-school arithmetic and into the ninth-grade arithmetic those who have shown the least progress.

Because a child can succeed in algebra is no assurance that he can profit by the course. He might find more useful the course in applied arithmetic. In educational guidance, the diagnosis of a pupil's ability must be supplemented with a diagnosis of his needs.

TOPICS FOR STUDY AND DISCUSSION

1. In the school system you know best, which status of the child is generally best served by the school, his legal status or his social status? (See the first principle.)

2. What is the justification of the compulsory attendance laws of a state?

3. If a state is limited in the amount of financial support that it can give to schools, is it justified in setting compulsory attendance to age 16, rather than holding it at 13 or 14 and thus better providing for the fewer classrooms to be supported?

4. List a few school practices that indicate respect for the worth of each pupil. List some that would seem to deny this basic principle of American life.

5. To what extent do standardized tests help teachers determine the normal child? To what extent have educators overemphasized this concept of the normal child?

6. What is the danger of overemphasizing the idea of differences among pupils?

Chapter 8

The Curriculum of the School

SOMEBODY HAS SAID THAT TEACHING IS A MATTER OF KNOW-
ing where you want to go and having a good means of
getting there. Knowing where we want to go represents
the purposes of education, and the means of getting there
represents the curriculum.

THE TEACHER'S PURPOSES

1. *One doesn't select a point of view of education as he
would pick out a new suit in a store.*

Treated in the first section of Chapter 3 were the broad
purposes of the American school. Any student of education, any teacher, will want to round out his own statement
of the school's position in American life, for a set of purposes is not something we build into our natures by mem-
orizing a statement set forth by another. One doesn't select
a point of view of education as he would pick out a new
suit at a store. Let's assume that the statement in question
can be taken as a typical one that a teacher might work
out in his own mind, from his own experiences; let's accept
it as a substitute pending time, experience, and desire of
the teacher to turn out his own directive.

The general purposes of the school serve to give a broad orientation to the teaching profession as a whole. The section just discussed serves alike for elementary teacher, high school teacher, college instructor, nursery school teacher, and teacher of adult or vocational courses. In additon, it may serve as a frame of reference or as a set of general standards against which a teacher may from time to time judge his own practices. It charts the broad and general course for schools and teachers, but it gives no specific directions.

2. *Behind any good curriculum are sound goals of education, firmly established with teachers.*

Specific purposes of education. For a quarter of a century or more teachers have been confronted with rather detailed lists of purposes of teaching and have become accustomed to participating in the development of such. At times it has been pointed out that purpose-stating can become an end in itself, if we don't guard against it, and that fine statements of good teaching intentions may not necessarily bring correspondingly good practices in the classrooms. There is, too, the danger of being too technical in building such lists. Although these dangers do exist, they should not discourage the practice of teachers charting their courses. There is no substitute for careful planning.

The words commonly found at the head of these lists are *purposes, outcomes, objectives,* and *goals,* with the adjectives *general* and *specific* used to make certain distinctions. To the writer, the three terms, purposes, objectives, and goals, can almost be used interchangeably, and there is little reason for committee members to get into an academic discussion about which is preferable. For convenience only, the writer is using the term purpose throughout this treatment. He might just as well have been talking about the goals of instruction, the objectives of education, the outcomes of teaching, or something else.

To explain the common practice that is followed in establishing lists of purposes, moving from the general purposes of the school (see section above) to the most specific purposes of a particular teacher, we can take the examples of three teachers working in the same school system, but teaching at different grade or subject levels. The variation in lists of purposes at their disposal might be as follows:

Primary Teacher	High-School Teacher of American Literature	High-School Teacher of World History

1. The Broad Purposes of the School in American Life

2. The Purposes of the Elementary School	2. The Purposes of the Secondary School	2. The Purposes of the Secondary School
3. The Specific Purposes of the Primary Program	3. The Specific Purposes of the English Program	3. The Specific Purposes of the Social Studies Program
	4. The Specific Purposes of the American Literature Course	4. The Specific Purposes of the World History Course

Examples of lists of specific purposes to serve particular fields of instruction are included below. These are not issued as either good, bad, or indifferent lists, but rather as typical examples of the work of teacher groups in trying to clear for themselves the direction in which they wished their instruction to go.

Outcomes of Reading Instruction in the Elementary Schools:

The child will enjoy reading.

He will turn to reading as one means of solving a problem, learning about things, learning how to do things, getting materials with which to think.

He will grow in ability to use reading skills.

He will formulate opinions based upon adequate and accurate sources of information.

He will recognize the possibilities, the dangers, and the limitations of printed materials.

He will learn to distinguish differences in quality with regard to beauty, truth, character.

He will accept his responsibilities to act as a member of democratic groups.

English Department Objectives

1. To acquire habits of clear, direct, forceful, and correct expression, written and oral.

2. To discover and develop special native abilities.

3. To learn to read silently with speed and accuracy.

4. To develop effectiveness in oral reading.

5. To enjoy wide (extensive) reading of good literature.

6. To learn to listen attentively.

7. To cultivate discriminating taste in the appreciation of radio and television programs, motion pictures, and dramatic performances.

8. To cultivate open-mindedness.

9. To read widely and discriminately from newspapers and magazines.

10. To acquire skill in collecting and organizing information from reference sources in the library.

11. To increase the use and understanding of words.

12. To correlate English with all other activities.

Social Studies Department Objectives

1. To build within the pupil a rational patriotism and a desire to maintain the democratic standards of our national life.

2. To instill in the pupil an appreciation of his rights, duties, privileges, and responsibilities as a citizen.

3. To acquaint the pupil with the communities of which he is a part, their conditions and their problems.

4. To impress the pupil with the necessity of co-operative effort in this world of increasing interdependence.

5. To develop within the pupil a loyalty for our basic institutions, with the understanding that they must be adjusted to changing conditions.

6. To train the pupil to select and weigh evidence with an open mind, so that he will think through social situations with truth as a goal.

7. To cultivate on the part of the pupil tolerance and a friendly attitude toward the customs, ideals, and traditions of other people.

8. To impress the pupil with his indebtedness to other people—past and present—in order to stimulate him to make his own contribution to progressing society.

9. To broaden and enrich the pupil's life through the awakening and growth of cultural interests.

10. To help the pupil to acquire the habit of considering the historical background of a' current problem in attempting to solve it.

11. To encourage the pupil to acquire the habit of reading extensively about social affairs.

12. To give the pupil an understanding of the economic system of which he is a part and to help him find a place for himself in it.

Nature of the Curriculum

3. The curriculum represents the total life of the school.

In giving full credit to the school for the influence that it exerts upon growing boys and girls, it would indeed be an understatement to say that all that these boys and girls carry away comes from the classroom program. The curriculum includes the total life of the school as it functions under the direction of teachers. This is not to underestimate the great significance of the classroom and its basic work.

Over and beyond the more formal activities of the classroom, also valued and encouraged in the modern elementary school are such activities as the traffic squad, the student council, classroom organizations, the clubs, the assemblies, the newspaper, the chorus, and hall, cafeteria, and similar service. The modern junior or senior high school duplicates these educational endeavors and adds a host of others. The educational program of the modern school would indeed be limited if it were pared down to the ·classroom work only.

The entire program that the school ·carries on in working with the students must be considered of educational value or possibility. Benjamin Franklin pointed out in setting up a school curriculum in 1743, "art is long and their

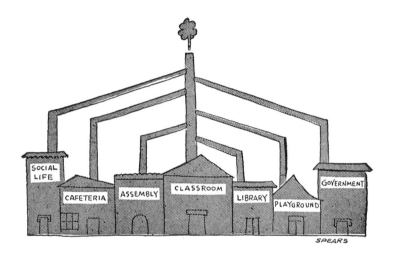

(the pupils') time is short"; the teacher needs to take educational advantage of all contacts with the pupils.

4. *The curriculum is something to be experienced, rather than something to be learned.*

Today, education is not conceived as something that takes place for eight, twelve, or any given number of years and is then complete. Instead, education is seen as a continuous life process, as the continuous growth of a person as he interacts with the life situations touching him at any moment, as he uses this study and experience to face tomorrow. Organized education, or schooling, proposes to help him make a more intelligent interaction with those life situations he is facing now and with those he will face later.

The future after-school situations of a person cannot be fully anticipated by a group of teachers and educators planning a school curriculum. These situations cannot be sufficiently determined to justify setting up a single body of content as material to be mastered to a specific degree by all. Of course most people will have certain needs in common, such as using numbers, expressing oneself adequately in writing and speaking, getting ideas from the printed page, and working co-operatively for the common good. But even in these areas, teachers must appreciate that such needs will vary greatly among citizens.

The test of learning comes in the active life situations of a person, there being a continuous chain of overlapping activities. Psychology has further pointed out that learning best takes place when the person is actively engaging in activities that he has accepted as meaningful. At the same time that the school sets up aspects of the curriculum more or less common to all, it provides active learning situations that will challenge the learner to bring out the best that is in him as he actively participates in this worthy work.

For instance, a fifth-grade unit of work built around correspondence with children in other parts of the United States can unfold into a miscellaneous but related lot of learnings, involving writing, reading, geographical concepts, history, oral expression, art, and what-not. How different from setting out five or six unrelated subject areas for attempted common mastery and stopping at that. The letter writing is a motivating factor used to stimulate the interest of the pupils. This activity with the information that it brought to the children about the various sections of the United States serves to enrich their learning experience in the life and the geography of their country, as well as to provide the opportunity for writing real rather than imaginary letters.

Any good elementary teacher appreciates the rewards that come from teaching arithmetic with manipulative materials and from applications of the more abstract learnings to living situations. The good high school teacher in a course in geometry invariably includes class experiences outside the building where geometry in action is emphasized.

The Pupil and the Curriculum

5. *The child does not want an easy school, he wants a challenging one.*

By nature children and youth are not lazy, they are active. If the teacher has any doubts about this, she need only watch them in their out-of-class and out-of-school activities. With but few exceptions they are busybodies who find the days too short.

They seem lazy in the classroom when they are matched with work that is out of the range of their ability and out of their sphere of interest. It is then that they seem dull. Some teachers are always complaining of their dull pupils. In these rooms are always found a fair percentage of inactive children.

Some teachers try to meet such situations by continually lowering expectations. Although it may be easier to lower one's expectations than to raise the standard of one's methods, the classroom may still remain dull for both pupil and teacher. An active child gets no more satisfaction out of the task too easy than he does from the task too difficult.

Some teachers have that rare quality of teaching that keeps all the class coming along, actively reaching for the accomplishments that seem just beyond them at the moment but yet within their range of achievement. This makes for a challenging situation. It is the interesting classroom, and not the easy one, that appeals to children.

6. *The student is more important than the subject.*

He deserves your sympathy; the subject doesn't—unless it is ailing and tottering around in an aimless manner. And even then, it invites improvement rather than sympathy. Subjects will always find their importance in the learner, not in themselves.

On the other hand, the old saying, "We are teaching children, not subjects," is an oversimplification of the situation we want. This saying means little unless we make the natural rejoinder, "We are teaching children *what?*" The what is our curriculum problem. In this century our profession has moved far in its appreciation of children's growth and development, but in doing so there should never have been any implication that the things to be taught were to be minimized. Rather, may we say, the subject matter of the schools today receives a more severe test than some years back, because there is so much more known about the child.

The teacher has much freedom in determining the nature of the courses he teaches; not even a basic textbook need crowd out his initiative and ingenuity. It is the responsibility of guidance to get a student into the class that seems to promise the greatest development and to change him from one room to another whenever the law of diminishing returns seems to operate to a degree that would invite such change. You may have little to do with a child's getting into your room, but you have a great responsibility for his direction once he is there. There is nothing of

ME FIRST, TEACHER

BAH!

THE STUDENT   THE SUBJECT

greater importance in your room than the individual pupil.

7. *The limitations of the specific subject that is being taught should never keep the teacher from sharing with his pupils the full breadth of his experience and the full richness of his personality.*

In our town, Nora, a teacher of eight and nine year olds, looks after her flock of thirty-five from 8:45 in the morning until 3 o'clock in the afternoon, exclusive of the lunch hour. In a nearby junior high school her sister Mary is a teacher of mathematics. The sisters have much in common, but they have one thing "in uncommon" that works to the advantage of the students of one and to the disadvantage of the students of the other.

Both teachers have master's degrees in their respective fields, both have traveled extensively, they have a fine cultural background in common, they are talented musically and play the piano equally well, they enjoy people, they are highly professional in school relationships, they both like teaching, and they are both highly conscientious about their work. However, Nora's students get full advantage of her interests and abilities, but Mary's students receive only a stilted portion of what she has to offer them.

With her lively group of normal eight and nine year olds, Nora directs a curriculum that encompasses a hundren and one learning activities and interests of children of that age. The facilities of her room are shifted and rearranged from time to time throughout the day, the week, and the year, as the varying needs of the occasion call for such flexibility of the room and of Nora. Both respond to the occasion, as the children day after day come to feel the charm and the talents of the teacher in "Miss Smith's room."

Over in Mary's room things move a bit differently. During the day five different groups of high school youth file in and then out of her room as they come for mathematics. The subject in itself is taught well and conscientiously, and the students respect the ability of the teacher in that field. Perhaps even respecting her ability are those who are failed each year, those who cannot profit by what Mary

is offering in her room, mathematics. Conscientiously she gives of only one portion of her many talents, for she was hired to teach mathematics, and she says she never has time to teach it as it should be taught. Her room is known by the students not as "Miss Smith's room," but as "the mathematics room."

The curriculum encompasses much more in learning possibilities than the subject itself. The subject is but one of the many means to the bigger ends of education. A particular teacher makes the difference between a rich classroom and a meager one. The teacher who feels the true depth of her calling, who places first the close human relationships that it implies, will see to it that the subject will not deprive her of sharing with her students the full breadth of her experience and the full richness of her personality.

8. *The limitations of certain pupils in such abilities as reading and writing invite the school to explore other possible means of securing and expressing ideas.*

There comes a time in the efforts of teachers when they must realize that some people will just have to go through life, and through the remainder of their schooling, somewhat handicapped in such fundamentals as reading and writing. But it must also be realized that such people will deal in ideas, concepts, and impressions, just as do the more capable readers and writers.

The school is invited to go behind its more formal program of reading and writing instruction to determine where it is trying to lead its pupils through such skills. Perhaps better citizenship, good work habits, the assumption of responsibility, sound health attitudes, and fine character are the things it is aiming at. Only by seeing clearly these ultimate goals can the school take a reasonable attitude toward the pupil who is going to continue to be limited in such skills as reading and writing. If it sees clearly these larger goals, the school will appreciate the fact that there are other aids to help pupils attain those ends. Radio, the motion picture, group discussion, transcriptions, field trips, the project approach to teaching, and other adjuncts to the printed page beckon for attention.

Limitations in reading ability in some children by the time they reach ninth or tenth grade level do not constitute a sin committed against teachers whose classrooms are loaded down with books. Such limitations are handicaps that should not deprive pupils of the right to reach their goals by means of other avenues.

THE FREEDOM OF THE TEACHER

9. *Most teachers have more freedom in determining what they teach than they seem to think they have.*

It is not uncommon for a teacher to rationalize his repetition of some unsuccessful teaching procedures with the statement that he is kept from changing by the administration, the state requirement, the college, the community feeling, the prescribed course of study, or the what-not.

So many different things can be done under the blanket head of a requirement, such as English 10, American history, or general mathematics. Even if *Silas Marner* is called for in the required English course, there is no reason that one teacher cannot limit the study to a week or two of extensive reading, even though the traditional routine would be five weeks of intensive reading. Even though American history is traditionally a chronological review of the political happenings from the exploration period down to the present, there is no reason that an enterprising teacher cannot capitalize upon the problems close to the lives of his students and their community and explore with the class the beginnings and the development of such problems through America's past.

Some beginning elementary teachers who tend to cock an overly suspicious eye at the school's practices of long standing, may shy away from the word-list approach to teaching spelling as though it outlawed teacher initiative. No alert teacher stops her instruction in spelling with the word list in the basic text. The techniques that a child develops in approaching the word list are recognized by the teacher, who in turn sees that the child uses them in attacking the spelling of other words within his experience. Certainly, practice in writing, which is so essential to spelling, is not limited to the words of the standard list. The teacher who thinks she is handicapped by the basic word lists is insinuating that learning to spell is merely a process of continually attacking strange words and storing them away for future use.

It is easier to imagine that we are prevented from doing a better teaching job than it is to do that better job.

10. *The subject is a means to an end, the end being the wholesome development of the pupil being served.*

The subject is not an end in itself, and it has no meaning without a learner to give it meaning. No more should be expected of a subject than it can actually contribute to the learning situation at hand. Should it become apparent that the pupil has little in common with a particular subject, it should not stand in the way of his wholesome development. That is, if it can't help him, certainly it should not be used against him. To fail a pupil because he has not profited by a subject, or to use the grade as a retribution may be to look upon it as an end in itself.

To attribute a disciplinary value to a subject, to tell the pupil that the reward for taking it rests in unrelated later life situations, or to evade otherwise his doubt of its value is to be unfair to both pupil and subject. Good teachers and schools will always depend heavily upon subject matter, but they will call upon it after instructional goals, student needs, and individual abilities and limitations have been determined—goals, needs, abilities, and limitations that reflect the present and possible future life of the pupil. And which pupil?—the one actually being served now, not the one who was here yesterday, not the one who will be here tomorrow, and not the one we would like to imagine is here today. Yes, a subject can help only the one who is here now. That's its test.

11. *The remedial approach to curriculum planning often violates sound principles of learning.*

The term *remedial* has been used glibly in the terminology of the American educator since about 1935. It was first used freely in labeling a special course for slower readers. Remedial reading as the title of a course for slow readers is still popular in many sections of the country. Remedial courses in other areas have also become popular with school administrators.

This remedial approach, as popularized since 1935, begins with the assumption that all children need and can

attain a common proficiency in such skills as reading, arithmetic, and spelling, and that the slow will respond to
repeated treatment. The remedial approach is to test for
the specific ability sought and to cut off for segregated
treatment those who fall below a certain proficiency.

Improving speed or comprehension in reading in the
beginning years of school is dependent upon challenging
experiences, not only with printed materials but also with
related activities leading up to and away from reading.
We must beware of looking upon reading improvement at
grade 7 or 9 or 10 as an isolated mechanical maneuver.
The improvement in reading, highly dependent as it is
upon the desire and the need to read, cannot be forced
upon a person. Sincere school administrators and conscientious English teachers must not let their interest in
the reading problem blind them to the psychological realities of learning.

This does not deny us the right to improve reading ability at these upper grade levels, nor the right to set up a
special class for it. It is merely a reminder that success will
be greater when these children are receptive to the course
and when the methods used respect the motivation techniques commonly used by good teachers in the grades
below. In other words, nothing automatic will happen
by segregating those pupils of lowest ability. The job calls
for a teacher who knows child nature as well as the more
intricate techniques of reading instruction.

Teachers at the junior and senior high school level especially must refrain from looking upon low reading ability
as an evil to be removed by a technical operation called
remedial reading. Perhaps the term remedial was an
ill-advised term to use for this enterprise of advancing

special means to help children and youth develop. The teachers of academic subjects at these school levels must first ask why does this child need to read better than he does? Is improvement in reading within the realm of possibility for him? Is he receptive to the idea? Or is it a school need instead of a pupil need that reflects fixed classroom requirements set beyond his ability?

Certainly good junior and senior high schools give their pupils help in improving their reading comprehension and rate, but such schools do so through regular classroom teachers who know something about the subject. There may be a specialist to help in the program, to draw children out for special instruction, with the aid of some special mechanical equipment, but such a specialist merely supplements the sensible and able approach of the regular classroom teachers. In other words, a remedial reading class should spur all language teachers to use improved techniques, rather than to relieve them of any further responsibility for improving reading ability.

SCHOOL CHANGE

12. *In educational planning there can be no progress without change, but there can be change without progress.*

Complacency or self-satisfaction will never assure a school the progress that it needs to achieve. Curriculum development is a continuous process of study and improvement. Changes must come regularly. They must be founded on careful study, research, and experimentation.

Even when change is made in some phase of the school's program, it must still be determined if progress has resulted. The true educational leader is one who is willing to back up and try again when it is apparent that the thing that seemed so promising is not paying the educational dividends that were expected. It is interesting for teachers to note the willingness of the medical profession to put into use a new drug that has seemed promising and to note the willingness of the doctors to back away from it when it doesn't live up to its promise or when something better is discovered.

13. *The improvement of the school's program must begin where the teacher is, just as learning in the classroom must begin where the pupil is.*

Now and then, school administrators are so imbued with a promising curriculum innovation that they have heard about or seen that they are tempted to put it into practice in their own schools almost at once. For instance, some years ago at the high-school level, the hour-period was adopted by school after school before teachers knew how to use it advantageously.

The idea called for a lesson or recitation part of the period and supervised study for the remainder. But the teachers were not at the true supervised-study level, and consequently many of them used that portion of the hour to do their desk work while the students studied. Others used the whole hour for recitation. They were not ready to use the active laboratory procedure upon which the success of the supervised study plan depends.

Some years ago the State of Virginia launched through its State Department what appeared on paper to be a most promising curriculum pattern for the local school systems. But the curriculum plan began where its designers were, not where the average teacher of Virginia was. Consequently, the classrooms of Virginia were not influenced to the extent that the printed course of study would imply. The state was never able to get from the new course the merits that were there.

A junior high school principal was once filled with the idea of a club for every student and every teacher. In one year he established 38 clubs in his school of one thousand students, a school that had had only 6 clubs the previous year. His teachers accepted the sponsorships at his bidding, but the spirit for clubs had not been developed. Within another year the program collapsed.

The wise administrator takes a sounding of the position of his staff before launching changes, and he wisely leads them from where they are.

14. *The teacher's smile or frown is as much a part of the curriculum as are the geography questions or the addition problems that are assigned.*

We cannot judge a school's curriculum by looking at the statement or the outline of it that is printed on a piece of paper. It can be judged only in the presence of the teachers who are introducing the program and the children who are experiencing it.

"I don't want Miss Doe next year," says the first-grader, "because she shouts at the kids." Even at the early primary years the children come to know through their companions which teachers shout, which are cross, and which operate their classrooms with a pleasant disposition. A smile on the teacher's face does not preclude efficiency and effectiveness of instruction.

It is not by chance that students at the upper grade levels assign pet names to those teachers who are severe, cross, or unreasonable. The child who has a pleasant and cheerful teacher takes much more away from the classroom for use now and in later life than does the child whose misfortune it is to have been placed with the teacher with a frown on his face and the world on his shoulders. The disagreeable teacher brings his out-of-school troubles into the school, is physically unfit, or is ill at ease with children.

15. *The heavier the percentage of failures at any grade level, or in any class, the more fixed is the curriculum.*

There is heavy evidence to show that not only are there breaks in our educational organization, but that teachers tend to be shocked at the pupils sent to them by the school below. The heaviest percentage of failure in school comes at the grades that represent the first in the respective school units.

That is, in the 8-4-4 plan, the heaviest percentage of failures in the elementary school comes in the first grade, in the high school at the ninth, and in the college at the freshman year. In the 6-3-3-4 plan the same thing holds true. In the 6-4-4-2 and the 6-6-4 plans, it is the same.

In other words, first, our school units tend to operate as separate entities and second, each tends to establish a fixed curriculum, which results in heavy failures at the first step of the new unit before pupils can make adjustments to that new school.

It has been stated by students of the subject that American schools fail about 20 per cent of the first-graders. Part of this failure is represented in the placement of some children in a so-called junior-primary class for a semester or a year before permitting them to enter the regular first grade. This heavy failure represents a fixed conception of the first-grade curriculum that has been handed down in America from earlier years.

In the case of the competent teacher who recognizes the natural differences among first-graders and adjusts her work and expectations in accordance with those differences, failures are at a minimum.

As to required high school subjects, English and mathematics usually take the heaviest toll. Again the curriculum is set out as a rather fixed body of content that must be mastered by all who dare pass that way. Only when work and expectations are set in reasonable relationship to capacity and needs can the curriculum be considered flexible and failures be held to a minimum.

In so far as teaching begins within a reasonable radius of the abilities of those being served by that teaching, the likelihood of failure is lessened.

16. *A school program does not stand still; it goes either forward or backward.*

The administrator who wants the maximum in learning from the school's efforts is wary of a static school program, highly organized to the point that the efficient organization becomes a joy and pride in itself.

For instance, the school that successfully operated 15 clubs last year finds this year that if such success is to carry over there must be some change in the club program.

Maybe 10 will continue, but 5 find a natural death because they do not fit the present situation, a situation which gives birth to a few new ones.

The forty-minute class period may have served the Horace Mann junior high school well for 20 years, but this year the pressure of a new instructional emphasis seems to call for one seventy-minute class period besides the shorter forty-minute periods.

Miss Jones' fourth-grade classroom, which carried out such a profitable unit on transportation last year, gives a minimum of attention to the subject this year, due to a particular combination of needs and interests in her new fifth-grade group. However, there is no reason to think that the year's program will not be just as successful as last year's.

Ordinarily Miss Ryan teaches first-grade each year. But last spring she asked to go with her group into second grade. It is quite possible that she will carry them through the third grade before she goes back to pick up a new first-grade class.

The curriculum is not a fixed piece of machinery to be polished and repolished each year until its gloss blinds the school and the community to its antiquity.

State Curriculum Directives

17. *It is not only highly interesting but absolutely essential that a teacher know the state school laws and regulations that govern his classroom teaching.*

Some of the most stimulating lessons in an undergraduate introduction-to-teaching course are those dealing with the school code of the state in question. Listed below are a few of the many state school laws of California that invite discussion of the legislators' intentions and the local school's obligations.

Protecting Rights of Pupils

Section 8271. No teacher in giving instruction, nor entertainments permitted in or about any school, shall reflect in any way upon citizens of the United States because of their race, color, or creed.

Section 8272. No textbook, chart, or other means of instruction adopted by the state, county, city, or city and county boards of education for use in the public schools shall contain any matter reflecting upon citizens of the United States because of their race, color, or creed.

Section 8273. No publication of a sectarian, partisan, or denominational character, shall be used or distributed in any school, or be made a part of any school library, nor shall any sectarian or denominational doctrine be taught in any school. Any school district or city, the officers of which knowingly allow any schools to be taught in violation of this section, forfeits all right to any state or county apportionment of school moneys, and upon satisfactory evidence of any violation, the Superintendent of Public Instruction and school superintendent shall withhold both state and county apportionments.

Elementary Curriculum

Section 10302. The course of study in the elementary schools shall include instruction in the following prescribed branches in the several grades in which each is required pursuant to this article: (a) reading, (b) writing, (c) spelling, (d) language study, (e) arith-

metic, (f) geography, (g) history of the United States
and of California, (h) civics, including a study of the
Declaration of Independence and of the Constitution
of the United States, (i) music, (j) art, (k) training
for healthful living, (l) morals and manners, and such
other studies not to exceed three as may be prescribed
by the board of education of the city, county, or city
and county.

Section 10303. A minimum of 50 per cent of each
school week shall be devoted to reading, writing, language study, spelling, arithmetic, and civics in grades
one to six, inclusive, and a minimum of 600 minutes
of each school week shall be devoted to such subjects
in grades seven and eight.

Citizenship Instruction

Section 10051. In all public and private schools located within the State, there shall be given regular
courses of instruction in the Constitution of the United
States, and in American history, including the study
of American institutions and ideals.

Section 10052. Instruction in the Constitution of the
United States shall begin not later than the opening of
the eighth grade and shall continue in the high school
course and in courses in State colleges, the universities,
and educational departments of State, municipal, and
private institutions, to an extent to be determined by
the Superintendent of Public Instruction.

Section 10053. No pupil shall receive a certificate of
graduation from any school described in Section 10052
unless he has satisfactorily passed an examination on
the provisions and principles of the United States Constitution and in American history. A student of college

or university who after having completed a course of instruction prescribed by this article and successfully passed an examination on the provisions and principles of the United States Constitution, and in American history, transfers to another college or university shall not be required to complete another such course or pass such an examination as a condition precedent to his graduation from the college or university.

Rule 97 (b). The governing board of the school district shall provide courses of instruction in American history and civics, including the study of American institutions and ideals and the Constitution of the United States, in length not less than 10 semester periods in every junior high school, senior high school, and four-year high school; and in every junior college for at least two credit hours.

Special Instruction

Section 8253. February 12th, the birthday of Abraham Lincoln, and February 22nd, the birthday of George Washington, are legal holidays. All public schools throughout the State shall hold sessions in the afternoon of the school day next preceding these holidays in order to allow the customary exercises in memory of Lincoln and Washington, respectively. When February 12th or February 22nd falls on a Sunday, the Monday following is a legal holiday and shall be so observed.

Section 8254. All persons responsible for the preparation or enforcement of courses of study shall provide for instruction on the subjects of alcohol and narcotics.

Section 10092. The governing board of each high school district shall prescribe a suitable course of fire prevention for all pupils enrolled in the day high school of the district.

Section 10093. The aims and purposes of the courses of fire prevention shall be as follows: (a) To create an understanding of the cause and origin of fires. (b) To emphasize the dangers of carelessness and neglect in homes and public buildings, and the necessity of care in the use of fires. (c) To promote an interest in preventing fires and the protection of lives and property.

Topics for Study and Discussion

1. If a teacher doesn't pick out a point of view or a philosophy of education, where does he get it? Do all teachers possess philosophies of education?

2. To what extent can a beginning teacher determine the curriculum that he is to follow in his classroom?

3. What is the relationship between a teacher's curriculum and his practices in marking the students?

4. What does the idea of a remedial class have in common with the teaching methods of good teachers who individualize instruction?

5. List the state school laws that act as mandates to the local schools in respect to the curriculum.

6. Account for the public interest that led to the passage of each of these laws.

PART III

Teaching—*From the Position of the Teacher*

Chapter 9

From Student to Teacher

THERE IS NO ONE EXACT PERIOD IN THE CAREER THAT MAKES or breaks the teacher. However, standing high in importance is that period in a teaching career that begins with the day that one steps into another's classroom as an assigned student teacher and ends when he closes his pupils' accounts on the last day of the first year in his own classroom.

It is a period to be packed with good sense, high courage, and professional—almost statesmanly—foresight. It constitutes a period of time overlapping college training and actual experience on the job. So similar are the opportunities and the pitfalls of student teaching and the first actual assignment that it is difficult to separate them in treatment. The period includes three major steps:

(1) Growing through student teaching (Chapter 9)
(2) Securing the first position (Chapter 10)
(3) Succeeding the first year in that job (Chapter 11)

Teaching—Never a Dull Moment

1. *The profound effort that one must put out from the beginning of student teaching to the close of the first year's assignment leaves him with the realization that success in teaching depends upon logical reasoning and hard work rather than upon quick thinking and so-called "tricks of the trade."*

None of the three steps above are to be taken lightly. Success as a student teacher may quickly become tarnished by the discouragement from not securing proper placement. Misplacement in the first assignment may temper success there. Failure in any of the three may affect noticeably the career to follow.

The Student-Teaching Period

2. *The climax of the training course for teaching is the period of directed practical experience in the classroom of a regular teacher.*

Every teachers' college or school of education provides in its training course a chance for the trainee to practice teaching in a classroom under the direction of a regular teacher. This experience comes usually during the last year of the training period, sometimes in the next to the last, and is offered as a course carrying credit for graduation. So fundamental is it, that state departments of public instruction refuse to grant a candidate a regular teaching credential unless he has passed such a course.

Usually this step in the training program is known as *student teaching.* In some sections of the country it is called *practice teaching,* and in others, *directed teaching.* Taken together, the terms student teaching, practice teaching, and directed teaching bear the same note of caution for the trainee, namely, that it is not quite the real thing. As great as the opportunity may be to try one's pedagogical wings, as these titles indicate he is still a *student,* he is still being *directed* by a more experienced person. It is after all a *practice* period in advance of the big game when he may carry the ball himself. Although no two student-teaching situations are alike (there being so many variables in them), out of the total experience of teacher training at this vital step in the program there have come some observations or pointers for the one who has not yet crossed that bridge.

Organization for Student Teaching. This phase of teacher training calls for a close working relationship between the training institution and the public schools in the geographical area in which the work is to be done. Invariably, public school systems assume their responsibility in the line of duty, realizing that education is a state responsibility and that only by helping to prepare teachers can they hope to secure them. The trainee needs to respect this contribution of the cooperating school and the sacrifice that is sometimes made as the school attempts to serve all the student teachers that the institution wishes to send out. Often a school is also serving one or more other training institutions, a situation which presents a definite complication.

Placing twenty, fifty, or two hundred and fifty students in practice teaching situations at any one time calls for astute manipulation. The college works through an officer with some such title as director of student teaching. To consummate the placement he must have at hand two sets of data, complete in every detail. The first comprises the information about the students who are to be placed. It is not as simple as listing the subjects or the grades in which they are to do their work. After all, they are personalities with strengths and limitations, some promising probable success in one type of situation and probable failure in another. Furthermore, where the geographical area of the total field of practice schools is wide, the trainees are bound to have preference of schools, because of convenience of transportation, home location, and other factors of consequence.

The other set of facts that the placement office must have clearly arranged comprises the list of practice schools, the potential student-teaching load each may carry, and a knowledge of the possible master teachers in each according to subject and grade. Furthermore, the more adequate the general knowledge of the school, the better can be the adjustment of student teachers in the placement.

3. *It is to the advantage of the training institution as well as to the student to effect his best possible placement in a student-teaching assignment.*

The trainee, who may be inclined to inject personal whims into his choice of school, master teacher, or whatnot, should appreciate fully the complicated mosaic that a college office has to piece together to find suitable practice situations for the whole crop of students. In placing his confidence in the placement office, he can rest assured that the official doing the placing is very interested in the trainee's success in the venture; failures not only call for more work in new adjustments but in the end reflect upon the college itself.

In colleges in which the classes are large, the student seldom has the opportunity to work directly with the director of student teaching. Instead, he works with a chairman or an adviser in his special teaching field, who in turn handles his case with the other office. Here again, close personal interest in proper placement is bound to be apparent. The experience of a college in its placement of student teachers should not be dismissed lightly by the student whose anxiety to succeed may lead him to make unreasonable requests.

As the college student nears the time to take a student-teaching assignment, it is quite natural for him to have some deep concern about the undertaking. At times such concern blossoms into anxiety, and the victim of such a case of student-teaching jitters turns for security to the people and the things most familiar. For instance, this pattern of thinking is not uncommon:

> There is his own high school, of which he'll always cherish fond recollections. In fact, right now the vision seems especially bright.
>
> And his U. S. history teacher, Mrs. Brown, was especially friendly. In fact, wasn't it she who had encouraged him to go into teaching?
>
> Isn't it strange that he is now seeking a chance to do his practice teaching in that same field of social studies?
>
> He has it! Why not do his student teaching under Mrs. Brown's direction?

There is no one correct answer to this question that arises with each class that goes out for the chance to practice what they have been learning on campus. The limited number of positions in some college situations makes it imperative for students to return to do their practice in the schools which they attended. However, where there is a choice of schools and classrooms, one's decision to return to practice in the school of his own youth should rest on ground more solid than that haunted by student-teaching jitters. The candidate for a teaching career must project himself into his future and realize that once beyond the practice situation he must be ready to tackle whatever kind of classroom comes his way. One must not pass up lightly the chance to attack student teaching in a strange school, under new conditions. It may pay great professional dividends later, even though at the moment it does not radiate the warmth of the home-town schoolhouse.

ASSIGNING THE TRAINEES

4. *Most helpful as a plan for student teaching is the assignment of a student to a school full time for a period of possibly twelve weeks to a full semester.*

There is wide variation among training institutions in respect to the period of student teaching. It is commonly agreed, although difficult to schedule, that the plan most helpful to the student is the one that sends him off campus completely for a period of twelve weeks to a full semester. Thus he has the opportunity to experience all aspects of the teaching situation, from the beginning of the day on the school playground to the closing after school with a faculty meeting, from the start on a Monday morning to the close on Friday evening.

Since the elementary teacher is one who must have proficiency in instruction in all the subjects—arithmetic, lan-

THE LIVES OF A STUDENT TEACHER

guage, social studies, science, reading, and so on, it is essential to secure a practice assignment that includes the miscellaneous activities of the elementary classroom. It is not uncommon to assign student teachers at this level to full-day, or at least half-day, schedules. However, at the secondary-school level, it is still quite common for the training institution to send the student out for a period or two of teaching a day in a nearby school, one so near that he can go back and forth between campus and high school, meeting a daily schedule of work in each.

Some institutions do not permit the difficulties of scheduling to keep them from giving their students a full-time assignment of practice teaching. A notable example of this is the state teachers' colleges of New Jersey. Regardless of grade-level of work, elementary or secondary, the student, at a certain point in his college work, closes the campus books and hangs out his student-teaching shingle on some public school of the state, where he works full time for twelve weeks. This period usually starts with the beginning of the last semester of training, thus allowing five or six weeks at the close of the period for some intensive work back on the campus, a program of work growing out of the experience gained from the practice situation.

Preparing the Student. Once the college has the schedule of student-teaching assignments arranged, it usually prepares the class for the work in the schools. Orientation often includes such topics of discussion and procedure as these:

1. A discussion of the proper dress for the assignment. It is at times difficult for a student to appreciate that the clothes of the campus are not necessarily the vogue among well-dressed teachers in the public school classrooms.

2. A consideration of the professional and ethical relationships of the student teacher to the principal and the teachers in the school to which he is going.

3. Advice from the outside. A superintendent, a principal, and an experienced teacher from the field may be quite helpful in speaking to a class, treating the practice-teacher's position as they see it from the other side of the fence.

4. An explanation of routine matters. There are always the records to be kept, the ratings to be given, the reports to make to campus in case of illness making necessary absence from assignment, and the materials to be taken to the training teacher. This is the routine procedure that calls for careful explanation and close attention.

5. A visiting day to the schools. On such a day the student teachers all go out to the schools in which they are to later do their practice teaching. The day enables them to become acquainted with the teachers, the classes, and the general procedures.

THE PUPIL'S PLACE IN THE STUDENT-TEACHING ARRANGEMENT

5. *The working relationship in any student-teaching assignment constitutes a triangular arrangement of the lines of communication and responsibility, with the student teacher, the training teacher, and the college supervisor stationed at the three corners, and with the class of pupils in the middle.*

Three people share the responsibility once the college student steps into a classroom to practice teaching: the student teacher, the supervisor from the college, and the training teacher in whose classroom the student does his stint. The training teacher is sometimes known as the master teacher or the critic teacher. Needless to say, the perfect situation is one in which there is mutual confidence all around, one in which the supposition that "two is company, three is a crowd" is outlawed.

No professional dividends will be paid if one of these possible arrangements is made at some time: (1) the student teacher and the training teacher determine that the

STUDENT   SUPERVISOR   MASTER TEACHER

THREE-PARTY LINE

supervisor is unfair; (2) the student teacher and the supervisor determine that the training teacher is unfair; (3) the training teacher and the supervisor determine that the student teacher is beyond help.

6. *The time that a student teacher may take to run to supervisor or training teacher for sympathy could better be spent in running to meet the educational needs of the pupils.*

One of the best assurances of an open and understanding relationship among the three parties is the provision of adequate supervision from the college. The supervisor needs to come around frequently enough to become well acquainted with the training teacher and with the work of the student teacher—to come around often enough to hold the confidence of both the other parties. Only by clearing responsibilities can the three give their best to the situation. Perhaps such responsibilities and limitations of the job can best be understood when the center of attention is upon the rights of the pupils.

7. *In any student-teaching situation, the responsibility is first to the child and next to the trainee.*

Only by fixing clearly in his own mind the important role of the child in the classroom can the student teacher see his own unique position in the scheme of things. Only by understanding clearly that the very existence of that classroom is to serve the education of the children can he understand the reluctance on the part of the training teacher to relinquish certain of the responsibilities to him. It is true that this master teacher owes a responsibility to the student in training, but this is secondary to the responsibility to the pupils. Which leads to this principle:

8. *By placing his mind on the needs of the children rather than on his own needs the student teacher can find his own most significant role in his assignment, and consequently profit most by it.*

The more the student teacher realizes that he is not the important one in the classroom, the less he is apt to feel that the master teacher is not fully appreciating him or his possible contribution. The author once surveyed the reactions of a statistically significant number of student teachers, after they had been out on the job for some weeks, to determine their chief reactions to their assignments. Although the majority were well acclimated to their situations, certain grievances appeared often enough to characterize them as the major probable disturbances that might be found in any group of practice teachers in any section of the country. The disturbed students were of these types:

1. The student teacher who feels that the training teacher doesn't give him enough to do, stays in the classroom all the time, and retains the main position.

2. The student teacher who feels that the training teacher gives him too much to do, takes advantage of him by giving him all the papers to mark and using the period as a free period.

3. The student teacher who finds the classroom in philosophy and practice to be much more conservative than the teachings on the campus led him to believe.

4. The student teacher who feels that the training teacher is resentful of the student teacher's popularity with the pupils.

5. The student teacher who feels that some of the staff of the school are unethical in their discussions of pupils, other teachers, and the profession itself.

6. The student teacher who feels that the college supervisor is not helpful enough, either because of infrequent visits, unreasonable expectations, or lack of practical suggestions.

REALISM AND RATINGS

Which may lead us to conclude that—

9. *The idealism that emanates from the campus of the training institution must be tempered with the realism of the classroom in which the practice teaching is to be done.*

All master teachers cannot be expected to find that happy medium between too much responsibility and too little responsibility for the student teacher. All supervisors cannot make all the visits that they would like to make from campus to school. All schools cannot be expected to have the modern curriculum that the beginner in the profession might believe desirable. All teachers in the field cannot be expected to possess the professional ethics for which we are still striving in teaching.

But this reality of the situation does not deny the beginner such rights as these:

1. The right to feel important in the student-teaching assignment, regardless of the amount of responsibility granted.

2. The right to grow through the assignment.

3. The right to study at close range the curriculum in operation, with thought of eventual alterations in his own future classroom.

4. The right to clarify his own code of ethics, as he reacts to the codes of others.

5. The right to improve his mechanics of human relationships as he deals with supervisor and training teacher.

10. *In every student-training assignment there are possibilities for the development of the student teacher if he keeps his eye on those possibilities instead of being blinded by the shortcomings of the situation.*

Reporting Progress. The responsibility for reporting the work of the student teacher is usually assumed by both the college supervisor and the training teacher. The college has a uniform system of rating that is used in all situations. It is common to have such reports sent to the college at intervals. For instance, at the Montclair, New Jersey, State Teachers College, during the period of practice teaching three such ratings are made out by each of two supervisors and the master teacher. One college supervisor is a subject specialist representing the student's major field and the other is a general supervisor. This rating card is reproduced in Table 6.

11. *Every rating made of a student-teacher's work should be discussed with the student teacher.*

As in all good supervisory practice, the persons doing the rating are encouraged to have conferences with the student teacher about the ratings at the time they are given.

TABLE 6

Student-Teacher Progress Report [1]

Name .... School ....

Evaluated by .... Date....... Hour......

The supervisor or training-teacher will place a check mark at the appropriate point on each scale. Since the student is permitted to see this card, the "suggestions" and "general comments" can be very stimulating.

_____

[1] Used at Montclair, New Jersey, State Teachers College.

TABLE 6—*Continued*

I. Personal Qualities:

Unsatisfactory	Satisfactory	Excellent

Poise; bearing; grooming; voice; use of English; forceful-ness; resourcefulness; enthusiasm; tact.

Suggestions:

II. Teaching Skills:

Unsatisfactory	Satisfactory	Excellent

Developing and clarifying objectives; arousing interest; securing sustained, coordinated effort; leadership; adaptation of materials to needs of individuals and groups; use of equipment and accessories; evaluation of results.

Suggestions:

III. Immediate Preparations:

Unsatisfactory	Satisfactory	Excellent

Systematic preparation of lesson plans; command of subject matter; provisions for rich and suggestive supplementary materials; relating the business of the hour to the events and thought of the day in community, state, nation, and world.

TABLE 6—*Continued*

Suggestions:

IV. Management and Control:

Unsatisfactory	Satisfactory	Excellent

Management of room and equipment; attention to individual needs; promptness and accuracy in routine; economy of time and effort; pupil citizenship.

Suggestions:

V. Professional Relationships:

Unsatisfactory	Satisfactory	Excellent

Cooperation with high school and college; acceptance of criticism and suggestions; ability in self-analysis.

Suggestions:

VI. Results:

Unsatisfactory	Satisfactory	Excellent

Attainment of objectives; growth of pupils; personal and professional growth of student teacher.

Suggestions:

General Comments:

12. *The values of student teaching need not be limited to those received in the classroom.*

Most teacher-training institutions encourage their students to look upon the assignment in the schools as the opportunity to participate in out-of-class activities as well as to practice teaching in the classroom. The breadth of the experience will depend upon such factors as these: the size of the school, the nature of the total program, the attitude of the administration, the length of the assignment, and also the inclination of the student to seek such extras. Such experiences as these are within the realm of possibility:

> Special help for small group or one child
> Service on the playground
> Service as a study-hall monitor
> Coaching dramatics group
> Club sponsorship
> Preparation of assemblies
> Observing faculty meetings
> Helping with supplies
> Accompanying children on field trip
> Attending parent-teacher meeting
> Attending board-of-education meeting
> Helping with carnivals or exhibits
> Assisting in sports and intra-murals

13. *Practice in understanding and getting along with other teachers, parents, and pupils is just as important as practice in teaching subject matter.*

The student teacher should take advantage of all opportunities to secure these extras from the school situation in which he finds himself. A supervisor once wrote upon a student teacher's rating sheet, "Increasingly friendly and sincerely interested in others," and in doing so emphasized one of the teacher's greatest possible attributes.

Internship in Teacher-Training. For many years educators have talked of the idea of adopting for their profession a period of internship that would reflect the faith that medicine places in the practice of internship. It would represent a more extensive period of practice than the present student-teaching period. Theory states that it might be a fifth year of training, spent in an actual school situation. Salient features of the arrangement would be:

1. The intern would be responsible to both the college and the school in which he would be doing his internship.

2. He would receive supervision from both the college and the local school.

3. He would gain experience in all the varied activities carried on by teachers.

4. His actual classroom load would be only a reasonable fraction of the teacher's normal load, to enable him to work gradually into the profession.

5. He would receive from the local school a salary appropriate to the duties assigned him.

6. He would be considered an associate member of the teaching staff.

7. The working arrangement would be covered by a contract between the college and the school, as well as by a contract between the intern and the local school district.

8. Special certification would be provided through the state department of public instruction, when necessary, to enable the intern to bear the responsibility for the supervision of children and the work handled.

9. Internship would be considered as the last step in the college's program of training and not as a method of giving relief to regular teachers in the schools using the interns.

10. The internship period would be no less than a semester, preferably a full year, and on a full day basis. It would come as the last step in the teacher-training program and would not replace the practices of observation and practice teaching provided earlier in the training.

As long as there is a shortage of teachers in the schools, it is doubtful if the few scattered programs of internship over the nation can be expected to multiply. Internship means the extension of the teacher-training period, and as long as there is a scarcity of teachers there is little hope of developing a more leisurely program of training.

In a few spots over the country a fifth year of training has been tried as a required part of the program. For instance, in most of the subject areas, the person who meets high-school certification requirements in California must take a five-year program. It is unfortunate that California has not seen fit to use that fifth year as a year of internship. In many universities, the influence of the special subject departments acts as a pressure to retain on-campus courses as the predominant means of training teachers.

Since American colleges have never shown either the readiness nor the agility of business and industry to effect changes readily in keeping with new ideas, it is quite likely that internship will continue only in the idea stage and that the present system of limited student teaching will retain its top position as the trainee's only classroom experience before entering a position.

Topics for Study and Discussion

1. Give evidences of the fact that teaching is dependent upon hard work rather than upon so-called "tricks of the trade."

2. Make a critical study of the organizational features of the student-teaching period as provided at the local institution—length of time, method of selecting school, provision for supervision, etc. Outline the most ideal student-teaching arrangement that a training institution might provide.

3. If a trainee fails in one student-teaching assignment, should another be arranged for him? If so, when should the shift be made?

4. Outline the help that a student teacher should expect to receive from the master teacher.

5. Is principle 7 fully acceptable as stated?

6. How much participation in out-of-class activities should be provided the student teacher by the school in which he carries out the student-teaching assignment?

7. Does internship have definite advantages over student teaching as a means of giving the trainee practical experience for teaching?

Chapter 10

The Chances of Employment

1. *The proper placement of a teacher candidate in a position is just as dependent upon the market as it is upon the candidate.*

The beginner seeking his first position casts himself into the teacher market, a market that is subject to the law of supply and demand just as surely as is the automobile or the pepper market. It can be said that the placement of a candidate in a position is subject to three general conditions:

(1) The teacher market
(2) The teacher's qualifications
(3) The conditions pertaining to the particular opening.

After adding to these three all the miscellaneous and chance factors that operate in the selection of teachers, it becomes apparent that the beginning teacher in seeking a position cannot expect to find the security of a commonly practiced set of sound principles of teacher selection.

THE SUPPLY AND DEMAND

In almost any school system at least 15 per cent of the

teaching positions become open jobs each year. In some instances, especially in small schools, as many as thirty or forty per cent of the positions may call for replacements each year. It is not uncommon to find two new teachers nearly every September in a small school employing a total of five or six. In the typical one-teacher school, of which America still has approximately 75,000, a new teacher is hired about every other year.

In a city the size of San Francisco, where nearly 1400 elementary teachers are employed, about 175 new teachers are needed each year in that department. In addition, about 125 other classrooms have to be covered by long-term substitutes to replace teachers on leave of absence for the year. Maternity, child care, business, health, and sabbatical leaves provide the need of replacements just as do actual retirements from the classrooms.

This going and coming among the teaching ranks reflects the natural laws of nature and the typical habits of mankind. The yearly demand for teachers can be summed up in these bare statements:

1. Some teachers die
2. Some retire because of age or ill health
3. Some resign to take other teaching positions
4. Some are promoted within the system
5. Some quit teaching to do other work
6. Some are dismissed
7. Some new positions are created.

2. *The long-term substitute position is not to be passed over lightly by the beginning teacher.*

Although they do not represent permanent openings, that is open jobs, to this list must be added those positions

FROM STUDENT TO TEACHER

vacated by teachers taking leaves of absence for the year. Many teachers get their foot in the door of a good school system by first accepting a long-term substitute position.

The yearly supply of teachers to fill these vacancies comes from the training institutions. Of course there is always a reshuffling of experienced teachers when vacancies occur, but when this rearrangement is completed the total number of openings still represents the total of the seven groups listed above.

To the yearly crop of beginners leaving the training institutions the profession looks for the material to fill up the ranks in the field. If the nation's open positions total 75,000 and the crop of beginners totals 125,000, the conditions of possible employment are quite different from a situation in which the beginners total only 30,000. This nationwide picture is altered in each state by the unique factors operating there.

For some years now, teachers coming out of college fully trained find themselves in a most favorable position for employment, providing they have given a little attention to the areas of greatest demand. For years, the number of newly trained teachers has not come near the number of openings. The slack is taken up by inadequately trained teachers who are granted emergency or sub-standard credentials. The greater the percentage of such teachers in the ranks, the more favorable the chances of good employment and advancement for the fully trained beginner, everything else being equal.

City Teachers and Country Cousins

3. *Statistics reveal that most beginning teachers find their first experience in a small school.*

This is accountable for three related reasons: (1) the great number of small schools, (2) the heavy turnover of teachers in small schools, and (3) the hiring practices of the cities.

Approximately 90 per cent of the nation's schools have no more than six teachers. In fact, a heavy percentage of these small schools employ only one, two, or three teachers. The turnover of teachers in the small schools is exceedingly heavy; each year 40 per cent of them are new to the job. This excessive exodus does not represent either failure of the teacher or impossible working conditions. There is no evidence to support the conjecture that there is a greater percentage of first-year failures among those who begin in the small school than among those who begin teaching in the city school. In fact, the movement of teachers from these positions follows natural causes.

The small school is usually found in the rural sections and in the small towns of a state, and usually salaries paid there are not commensurate with those paid in the cities. Everything else being equal, an experienced teacher can secure a higher salary than a beginner. Furthermore, in times when there is no shortage of fully trained teachers, the cities have been inclined to employ only those candidates who have had two or three years of experience elsewhere. The better salaries paid, plus the American inclination to migrate toward metropolitan areas, have enabled cities to follow this employment policy. Regardless of its merits, this condition where it does exist tends to send the beginner into the country for his first assignment.

The writer's experience in both metropolitan and rural areas leads him to advance, in the absence of statistics, the possibility of one other condition to account for part of the heavy exodus of teachers from the small rural schools. The story goes like this: To begin with, the preponderance of new teachers each year in these schools are young women. The small town or the rural community presents the young woman teacher an excellent opportunity to build up social relationships in the community. When she takes the job she doesn't have to do anything unusual to be noticed. On the sidewalks, in the village church, or in the country store, there are no crowds to hide her identity. And the statement, "There goes the new teacher," is just as natural with the natives as one about the weather or the crops. Consequently, with these social contacts come opportunities to meet men eligible for marriage. It is generally known that a number of the teaching openings in the country each year are a result of the natural inclination of young women to exchange their professional career for one in home-making.

This combination of social contacts with the teaching position, so common in small towns and rural areas, is in decided contrast to the situation in the large city. There the new teacher is often swallowed up by the existing complications of metropolitan existence, where her identity as "the new teacher" is limited in geographical sphere to the particular school in which she is teaching and to the small group of professional associates that she meets on the job. It is not the writer's intention to glamorize for the beginner the teaching position in the rural area at the expense of the one in the city. It is merely to throw in this note to counteract the overworked supposition that the position in the country is one of isolation for the beginner. Who is to say that the stranger in the city is not one of the loneliest people in the world? Who is to say that the newcomer to a very small community is not soon to be a person with the richest friendships?

The Experience Requirement. Just because city systems often discriminate against the inexperienced teacher is no reason that the practice should be encouraged. The National Education Association, always the friend and guardian of the rights and welfare of the teacher, made itself clear on this point over a quarter of a century ago with this statement:

> It is customary for some cities to require teaching experience as a pre-requisite to election to teach. This practice has the approval of tradition. There is no other justification for it except that cities making this requirement usually pay salaries enough higher than those in other places to enable them to enforce this regulation. It is not desirable and should not be necessary for the school authorities in one district to insist that young and untrained teachers secure their first experience at the expense of the children of another district.[1]

Where such a requirement does exist, it challenges the beginning teacher to look ahead at his career and plan carefully the steps that he hopes to take throughout the formative years. There is no substitute for experience in teaching, and certainly no substitute for teaching in varied situations.

What the Teacher Has to Sell

4. *The teacher seeking a position has something to sell, and to this something a price can be fixed.*

---

[1] *Teachers Salaries and Salary Trends.* National Education Association, 1923, p. 48.

Over and beyond the general nationwide conditions that influence both the possibility of employment and the salary level, are the specific conditions pertaining to the teacher in question and the job opening at hand. Although the code of ethics of the profession might seem to indicate otherwise, the bare fact remains that to a marked degree the employment of a teacher represents a bartering proposition, in which the worth of the teacher is being weighed against the value of the position. In a sense, a teacher seeking a position bears an invisible price tag.

As indicated previously this price reaches a certain level because of statewide or nationwide conditions over which the teacher seeking a job and the local employer seeking a candidate have no immediate influence. For instance, when Indiana by state legislation placed $2400 as the minimum salary of teachers in that state, this represented a price below which neither individual teacher nor individual employer could go in their bargaining. Needless to say, Indiana adopted this favorable legislation in the late forties when teachers were scarce.

The teacher seeking a position has something to sell and a record to indicate the value of this something. The possible value of a teacher is represented by these things:

1. The amount of professional training, with special reference to the relationship of that training to the specific position being considered.

2. The personal qualifications for teaching, as represented by personality, health, age, and freedom from outside obligations that might distract from attention to the job.

3. Experience in the work or in related activities.

4. The record made in training and experience.

The one seeking a position must be reasonable in matching his own qualifications against the requirements of the opening. To an employer seeking a primary teacher, five years of specialized professional training in music instruction will not look as good as two or three years of professional training aimed directly at primary education.

The person seeking a position must try to be honest with himself about his personal qualifications. For instance, many school systems require health examinations of teachers, and those that don't still expect good physical performance on the job. As to a good personality for teaching, this is reflected in one's papers of recommendation as well as in one's personal contacts and appearance in the course of the interviews for employment. The absence of a natural love for children or a desire to be with them may crop up in one's papers in the lack of any voluntary experience with them.

Extra Experience. As to experience in the work, the beginner must substitute the student-teaching assignment or related activities with children as evidence of competence. For this purpose, a good record in student teaching is as

SUPPLY—AND—

fine for a beginner as a good record in actual teaching is for the person of experience who seeks better employment. The one who makes a poor record in student teaching needs to realize the handicap that it may be in securing good employment. This is not to say that poor performance in the student-teaching situation is always the fault of the student. Rather, it is to say that there is no other experience record for the beginner to present, a fact which magnifies the importance of this practice experience with the employer.

The student in training who by some technicality may have the chance to avoid student teaching needs to realize how the lack of such a record may hinder favorable employment. For instance, many students who trained first for high-school teaching and did their student teaching in a high school, have later taken some elementary training to qualify for that field. Invariably the employer for an elementary position is more impressed by such a candidate if this later training also includes student teaching at the lower level.

The record one makes in the training institution and in

DEMAND

the student-teaching assignment is of great consequence in securing a position. In the days of teacher shortages, a weak college record may not keep a beginner from securing a position, but quite likely it will keep him from securing the position that may be most attractive.

It is common knowledge that the graduates with the most promising records can command the more favorable positions if they approach their placement in the same sensible manner that they used in attacking their training. This calls for an attitude of reasonable assurance rather than one of utter independence.

What the School Has to Offer

5. *Among candidates for teaching positions, salary and location of the position both rank high in the list of major concerns.*

Location of the Opening. The typical woman teacher who comes from a rural area or a small town is willing to take a position some distance from home. This may be accounted for in three ways: (1) that the person expected to have to do so when she began her training, because the teaching positions in her home community were so limited in number; (2) that she left home to attend a training institution and thus broke the family ties sufficiently to leave home to teach; and (3) that she is attracted by the better salaries in larger school systems.

The typical woman teacher who comes from a large city is reluctant to leave home to accept a position. Training is often obtainable in the home area, attendance necessitating little more than commuting by bus or automobile. There being so many teaching openings in the home city each year, she often takes it for granted that there is a favorable chance of securing a position there. When he was at Montclair, New Jersey, State Teachers College, the author saw many women students from Newark turn from teaching after securing the training just because they could not secure a position at home or within commuting distance. Likewise, in the San Francisco Bay area, most of the young women who go to one of the four or five teacher training institutions in their immediate vicinity would never think of seeking employment in other sections of the state.

Generally speaking, the young man who enters teaching is much more mobile, regardless of his home background. Perhaps the experience of the race bears out this tendency of the male to roam a bit more than the female, to stray from the nest sooner.

And so it may be said that one important feature of the position that a local school system has to offer is one over which it has no control—the location. However, what a school lacks in control here it can make up for in its control over salary. The more principles of sound salary policy that are followed, the more chance a school system has of attracting good teacher candidates:

1. The salary policy of a school system should be outlined in systematic form in a salary schedule, listing such uniformities as beginning and maximum salaries and increments.

2. It should recognize the principle of equal pay for equal service.

3. The policy should make distinctions for training and experience, but not for grade level, sex, or race.

4. In attracting candidates, the school should not dis-

criminate against a person because of residence, marital status, sex, race, religion, or color.

5. The salary policy of a school system should enable its teachers to make a living adjustment to the school community that is in keeping with their professional training, that respects the level of their social responsibilities, and that is conducive to good teaching.

6. It should encourage continued professional growth and maximum teaching contribution while in service.

7. In attracting competent personnel, the school district must naturally recognize variations in teacher markets and in economic conditions from time to time.

8. The salary policy followed must be specific enough to enable beginning teachers to see rather clearly their possible salary positions in the years to come, but at the same time it needs to be flexible enough to enable the school to provide for the variations necessary to effect the standards set out in the principles listed above.

The candidate need not expect to find all of these principles operating in very many of the school systems that may interview him for positions. On the other hand, as a student of education he can get professional satisfaction out of the fact that each year a greater percentage of school systems are turning in the direction of these principles.

THE SALARY SCHEDULE

6. *Morale among teachers in a school system is promoted by the existence of a definite salary schedule that recognizes sound policies.*

Needless to say, school systems vary widely in their salary policies. The feature that they have in common is the percentage of the total school budget that is devoted to salaries. It is common for about two-thirds of school revenue to be paid out for salaries.

Salary schedules are found more frequently in cities than in villages and rural areas. About two-thirds of the cities of the country maintain salary schedules.

Some years ago it was common practice to pay higher salaries to high school teachers than to elementary school teachers of equal training and experience, but during the past decade there has been a heavy trend toward the single-salary schedule, which makes distinctions not on grade-level taught but on experience and training. Teaching in the elementary school has rightfully taken its place on a level of importance with teaching in the upper school. Some of the most significant instruction comes in the early years of schooling.

Some school systems still discriminate against married women in the selection of teachers, but this practice is rapidly being discredited. Only when outside work detracts from competent service in the school should the employer become concerned. The board of education, in contracting for a teacher's time, does so for only that portion of his time necessary to carry out the job efficiently. To carry out the contract in this spirit places obligations upon both employer and employee.

In Table 7, we see a single-salary schedule. The movement up the scale is automatic, each additional year of service meaning one higher step until the teacher reaches the maximum salary. Naturally, there are many variations of these basic features of a salary schedule. For instance, some school systems make movement on the scale dependent upon in-service study. A few scales include a third lane for teachers having completed the doctorate work or the equivalent.

7. *The candidate seeking a position should not let the brilliance of a good beginning salary keep him from noticing the provisions for financial advancement in the system.*

Often a school system pays high beginning salaries in order to compete with other communities, but fails to provide much advancement beyond the beginning salary. When the author worked for an Illinois township school board some years ago, the board paid very high salaries to some teachers but provided no assurance of a teacher arriving at those top positions. The board did not believe in a salary schedule.

When no definite scale with automatic increments is in evidence, it is sound business for the candidate to determine the existing salary policy in the school system. The candidate's consideration of a position is in a sense a possible union of teacher and school system, and the teacher has as much right to find out about the school as the school to find out about the teacher.

The beginner needs to realize that every school system has a salary policy and that in many school districts it is nothing more than a hit-and-miss bargaining, reflecting the momentary opinion of the superintendent or school trustee who is in the position at the time contracts are issued for the new year. Because of other factors in the situation, the candidate may still wish to accept a position under such circumstances. However, he deserves all the facts before making a decision.

8. *The candidate for a teaching position needs to realize that possible positions cannot be compared on salary alone.*

Just as the teacher seeking a position has something to sell, so does the school system seeking a teacher have something to offer. It is up to the candidate to determine as fully as possible exactly what it is that a position offers. The salary is only a portion of the offer.

TABLE 7

A Single-Salary Schedule

Step	A.B. or B.S. Degree	Master's Degree
1	$2400	$2700
2	2600	2900
3	2800	3100
4	3000	3300
5	3200	3500
6	3400	3700
7	3600	3900
8	3800	4100
9	4000	4300
10	4200	4500
11	4400	4700
12	4600	4900
13	4800	5100
14	5000	5300
15	5200	5500

The teacher advances a step on the scale each year in service, and can move from the first division to the second when he completes the Master's degree. The table serves all teachers in the system, regardless of grade-level placement.

An initial contact with a school system often gives an insight into the possible working conditions. The degree of professional and business-like approach reflected by the employing office has its influence upon the candidate. Among the outward evidences of a school organization that respects professional ethics and accepted principles of sound school procedure are these:

1. The superintendent is responsible for nominating all new employees, and the board of education elects only upon his nominations.

2. The school system has a salary policy that can be shown to the candidate. For instance, the salary of the position in question is represented in the policy, any possible variation in the salary being due to such usual provisions as variation in experience and training of the candidates.

3. The employing office reveals interest in the candidate's professional qualifications, rather than in his religion, race, color, residence, or marital status.

State Regulation of Employment

9. *The standards of teacher appointment, as followed by a local school system, are subject to state law but may go beyond it.*

For instance,

1. Many states set a minimum salary for a teacher who has four years of professional training.[2] Such figures are altered upward from time to time. For instance, California's former minimum has been replaced with $3400.

---

[2] See *Teachers in the Public Schools.* National Education Association Research Bulletin, 27:4, 1949, p. 143.

Local school systems often go beyond such a state mandate when they set the lowest salary on their schedule.

2. A local school system cannot appoint a teacher who is not certified by the state's licensing bureau, but it may set its standards or regulations higher than the state's if it wishes. School systems often set requirements in regard to marriage, sex, place of residence, and age.

Certification. The certificate does not guarantee employment but marks the teacher as an eligible candidate. The state sets out the requirements and administers the certification. If a teacher crosses a state line he goes through the process again with the new state department of education to secure his credential.

AVENUES OF EMPLOYMENT

10. *That a teacher secures the right position, and a school system the right teacher for the position is the goal of teacher placement.*

11. *Regardless of how well teachers are trained, the effectiveness of their work is dependent upon proper placement.*

Consequently, it behooves the candidate to study closely the various aspects of an opening, matching his own qualifications and nature against the requirements and the working conditions. At the same time, proper adjustment of teachers to jobs behooves the school system to study closely the qualifications of a candidate in relationship to the position that is open.

Most fortunate is the candidate who is told the job specifications of the position. Surely if the school superintendent, or his assistant, knows what the job is that he is trying to fill he can pass the details on to the candidate. For instance, if it is an elementary position, what grade level is it? Are there any additional duties or any unique situations connected with the position? If it is a high school position, what subjects are involved and what extra-curricular activities are included?

College Placement Bureaus. Most beginning teachers secure their first positions through the cooperation of their own training institutions. Some months before a class

PLACEMENT
BUREAU

graduates, the institutional placement office adds the new class to its files. The "papers" of each are assembled, usually with photographs, and are made available to prospective employers. In the papers of a candidate are data sheets giving the facts and statements or rating sheets setting out the opinions of instructors, master teachers, and college supervisors. Included in the data sheets is such information as name, age, address, courses taken, type of certificate, degrees, and special interests and abilities.

With school officials experienced in the selection of teachers, one can always get an interesting discussion of the merits and shortcomings of the letter of recommendation and the rating sheet. It is true that they reflect the variables of personal opinion, both from the angle of their authors and from the angle of their readers. Most college placement offices prefer to bring the employer to the school, where interviews with the candidates are held. The papers may have been sent out to the superintendent, before he comes to the interviews, or he may pick up afterwards the papers of those candidates in which he is most interested.

The placement officer is more than a collector of papers and an arranger of interviews. He often acts as an adviser to both candidate and employer. He sees the teacher market as a whole, he knows the habits of school administrators, he knows the background of teaching in the various communities, he sees the area of greatest shortage and those in which placement is difficult, he has a good opinion of a fair beginning salary—in short, he can be of great service to a beginner. He is a professional leader who feels a responsibility to both teacher and teaching.

Other Placement Bureaus. Besides the college placement office, placement services are often provided through state departments of education and state teachers' associations. Before all of these professional agencies were set up, teachers seeking employment depended largely upon their own personal applications and upon commercial agencies. The latter, in the case of a placement, follow the practice of charging as a fee a certain percentage of the candidate's first year's salary. Due to the courtesies extended by the college and the college's ready access to correct and unprejudiced information about their candidates, employing officials usually go first to the college when hiring inexperienced teachers.

Large Systems. In the large school systems where scores of new teachers are employed each year, it is common for the candidates to be scheduled to oral interview and at times to written examination. In hiring elementary teachers, one large school system uses this procedure:

1. The need of teachers is announced to the colleges and through the press. The dates of interviews and examinations are made known.

2. The candidates make out their application blanks.

3. The personnel director of the school system collects the papers of the candidates from the colleges.

4. The dates for oral interviews and written examinations are set and the candidates notified.

5. The written examinations, taking two hours, are given at two different times for convenience of the applicants. Adjustments in the interview schedule are likewise made for their convenience.

6. The oral interview is conducted by a board of three principals and supervisors. After the interview each of the three fills out a rating sheet, and the interview score is the average of the three. The papers of the candidate are taken into consideration by the board as they attempt to judge the candidate's competence to fill the positions open.

7. The personnel office then combines the scores of the interview and the written examination for each candidate and compiles all names on a list from highest to lowest score. Below a certain point on the scale, candidates are considered as having failed. The others are notified that they have been placed on the eligible list.

8. Should there be two hundred on the eligible list when one hundred positions are to be filled, the first one hundred on the list are offered positions. In the case of

rejections, the employer goes on down the list until he secures the teachers needed.

9. The list may be used for an entire year. Interviews and examinations are held some months later, and new names are fitted into the list at their proper levels.

10. Near the end of the year the list is abolished, and those who were never hired have the privilege of going through the examinations and interviews again to attempt to make the new list.

Although some aspects of such a procedure may seem somewhat mechanical, teachers generally appreciate the protection that they receive through the rating system leading to placement on a list. The high recommendations that they bring from the college and their student-teaching experience are bound to influence the interviewing board of a large city just as they would the superintendent in a small town who has only two positions to fill.

The National Teacher Examinations. Available to school administrators, in their attempt to select candidates with competencies essential to successful teaching, are the National Teacher Examinations. Administered annually on a national basis, these examinations are designed to provide objective measurements of certain abilities and knowledge of teachers.

The scores on these tests are to be used in conjunction with records of experience, academic records, interviews, and recommendations and ratings by qualified observers. The examinations are sponsored by the American Council on Education and are administered by Educational Testing Service, usually in February. They are given in a number of centers throughout the United States. Colleges of education often act as centers, and thus encourage their own outgoing students to secure test scores for possible future use in securing employment.

The Common Examinations are designed to measure knowledge and ability, and include tests in these fields: General Culture, Verbal Comprehension, English Expression, Nonverbal Reasoning, and Professional Information. Approximately four and a half hours is set aside for the Common Examinations.

In addition to the Common Examinations, the candidate may choose one or two additional tests from the Optional Examinations, in keeping with the field in which he expects to teach. An hour and three quarters is devoted to each of these. The fields represented are:

1. Education in the Elementary School
2. Biological Sciences
3. English Language and Literature
4. Industrial Arts Education
5. Mathematics
6. Physical Sciences
7. Social Studies
8. French
9. German
10. Spanish
11. Latin

The candidate secures his application blank from his college, the school system to which he is applying, or directly from Educational Testing Service, P. O. Box 592, Princeton, New Jersey. Non-student candidates pay $10 to take the examinations, and student candidates pay $6. Approximately 125 teacher training institutions act as centers, in addition to the city school systems that administer them to their own candidates.

The student candidate's test scores are reported to him and to his college if he wishes. The non-student candidate may have his sent to his college and to one school system.

Since this examination service was first inaugurated in 1940, it has gained steadily in popularity. As school systems continue to search for more objective aids in the selection of their candidates it is natural for examinations to play their proper role.

12. *The extent to which a teacher seeking a position needs to go from school door to school door to secure it depends upon the market.*

Applications. If the teacher has a good record and is certified in a field in which there is a scarcity of teachers, the opening will seek out the teacher. If the teacher has a mediocre record and is in a field in which there is a scarcity of teachers, he may or may not be sought out. If he has a good record and is in a field in which there is no scarcity, he is apt to be noticed. If he has an average or lower record and is in a field in which there is no scarcity of teachers, it would do him well to exert much time and energy to the task of making direct contacts with schools to determine if he might secure placement.

Almost every training institution, during the last term of the student's work, gives some attention to the techniques of making both written and face-to-face contacts in applying for a position. Most superintendents can show a student examples of the types of letters that they should not write in seeking employment. It is indeed surprising how some candidates with promising records are willing to make their first impression with a poorly written letter of application.

THE TEACHER'S CONTRACTUAL STATUS

When the beginning teacher accepts a position and thus removes himself as a candidate in other school systems, he must have something in writing to seal the bargain. Often the first notification of appointment is by letter, which indicates that the contract will follow. In a few school systems governed by tenure regulations, the school considers that the letter legally constitutes the appointment with all the rights of contractual status. If a letter notifies the person of appointment and sets out the basic specifications of the employment, such as salary and dates of the school year, no doubt this would suffice. However, most school systems use contract forms, mailing two to the appointee with directions to sign and return one to the employer. That employment status be set forth in writing is school law in most states.

Once the teacher has given his word to a school that he will accept the position, unless the actual appointment alters the proposed conditions of employment, it is the candidate's professional obligation to keep his part of the bargain. A beginning teacher who is a candidate for more than one position should realize that a more attractive offer might still come through after he has given his word to accept a given position.

13. *It is a candidate's professional right to hold out as long as he wishes, but it is his professional obligation to accept an appointment once he has told the employer that he will do so.*

When there is no state law requiring a written statement of employment, an oral contract is usually considered valid.

Since a beginning teacher can hardly be expected to know all of the statutory regulations pertaining to employment, it is best to ask for a written statement of employment.

In many states a standard contract form is prepared by the state department of education and made available to local school systems. In as many as a fourth of the states its use is mandatory.

The employment of the candidate is made with the understanding that he can meet the certification requirements. Even though he may render the service or any portion of it, he cannot recover the salary or other benefits of the position unless the requirements of certification are met and the credential is received and filed by the proper date with the local school system.

Further Study. A number of enlightening bulletins treating the selection and appointment of teachers and the conditions of employment and advancement have been issued by the National Education Association and can be secured from the Washington office. Among the series are these which should be of interest to a beginning teacher:

1. *Teacher Personnel Procedures: Selection and Appointment,* Research Bulletin, Vol. 20, No. 2.

2. *Teacher Personnel Procedures: Employment Conditions of Service,* Research Bulletin, Vol. 20, No. 3.

3. *Teachers in the Public Schools,* Research Bulletin, Vol. 27, No. 4.

Some of the more apparent ethics of teacher placement might be summed up in these principles:

1. The right candidate in the right position should be the goal of the candidate, the employer, and the placement officer.

2. Candidates should be placed on no basis except merit alone.

3. The machinery of placement should protect the time and the efforts of candidate and employer alike.

4. There should be a mutual respect of the confidential nature of recommendations and other papers of application.

5. Teachers should not have to bid or to bargain for positions.

6. When a vacancy is filled, all candidates should be notified of the action at once.

7. Neither the candidate nor the employer should resort to high-pressure tactics.

8. Candidates should make their applications through the office of the superintendent or his assistant appointed to that duty.

TOPICS FOR STUDY AND DISCUSSION

1. This chapter emphasizes three or four general conditions that influence the placement of a candidate in a teaching position. Bring these down to specifics in your geographical area to show the interplay of these conditions.

2. Review the teacher market in your geographical area at the moment, emphasizing and matching the supply of teachers and the demand for teachers.

3. Review practices relative to the employment of substitute teachers as these practices operate in the schools known to members of this study group.

4. Why do so many beginning teachers secure their first experience in small schools? Is this desirable?

5. Make a list of the teaching potentialities that you have to sell to an employer in securing a teaching position. Be objective; do not list generalities.

6. Describe the type of position you wish to secure and match your qualifications (5 above) against the position.

7. To what extent should salary policy influence an applicant in accepting a position?

8. Review the helps to employment open to a teacher graduating from the local institution.

9. Write a letter of application for a teaching position.

Chapter 11

Succeeding on the First Job

DEEP IN THE HEART OF EVERY BEGINNING TEACHER IS A
driving desire to succeed on the first job. There is nothing
as exhilarating as early success and nothing as discouraging as early difficulties.

A typical group of 125 new teachers who had just completed their first year came through the experience with
these three suggestions for those who had not yet entered
their first assignments:

>*Be firm but fair from the beginning*
>
>*Know your pupils*
>
>*Plan your work carefully.*[1]

Although they considered these three points the key
to a good start in the profession, they added these rules
as likewise aids to success for a beginning teacher:

>Observe other teachers
>
>Don't hesitate to ask questions
>
>Be friendly with other teachers
>
>Be calm
>
>Be prompt with clerical work

---

[1] "Spotlight on Inducting New Teachers," New York City bulletin,
Curriculum and Materials, Vol. 5, No. 1, p. 3.

OBSERVE OTHER TEACHERS

COLLECT MATERIALS

BE CALM

ESTABLISH. GOOD ATMOSPHERE FOR LEARNING

PLAN CAREFULLY

PLANS

PLANS

SPEARS

Start slowly
Get to school early
Establish routines
Collect materials for later use
Be consistent
Be patient
Use pleasant voice
Read professional literature
Don't do clerical work in class
Accept and apply suggestions.

No doubt, a group of experienced teachers and administrators would have about the same pointers for beginners. Instructors on the college campus would not stray far from this list. But perhaps the really good principles of teaching become more meaningful to a person after he has experienced a classroom of his own.

It is easy enough to accept in theory the idea that good classroom control is dependent upon being firm, fair, and friendly. But how many start their classrooms with a fear of firmness because of the greater fear of not being liked by their pupils? Many a teacher starts the job with the firmness without the fairness, and many others start with fairness without the firmness. Trying to backtrack and recover the fumble is much more difficult than following the reasoning of the 125 New York teachers—"Be firm and fair *from the beginning*."

Securing a Good Atmosphere for Learning

1. *The big difference between the first actual teaching position and the student-teaching assignment is the absence of the control exercised by an experienced teacher.*

A teacher, after being on the first job for about a month and still unable to control his class, told one of his supervisors that he was sure he could teach children something if only they would pay attention. This sad commentary would lead us to believe that he looked upon classroom control and classroom teaching as separate enterprises.

Highly successful in a student-teaching situation, his loss of control in his own classroom reflected the absence of the control exercised by a master teacher. Perhaps in the student-teaching situation he had misjudged the influence that the master teacher exerted upon the class even when out of the room. His commentary indicated that he failed to see that securing the proper learning atmosphere in the room is just as much teaching as explaining sentence structure and mathematical processes.

Of the group of 125 teachers mentioned above, 73 indicated that discipline was the major problem of adjustment in their first assignments. They characterized their troubles with such statements as these: too many problem children, pupils did not respect authority, I failed to train the class in work habits, and I had had no experience with problems.

One of these confessions admits the teacher's failure to establish work habits. However, between the lines in the others we may read such possible failures as a lack of planning for *all* the pupils, the lack of knowledge of all the pupils, and the absence of firmness in those important first days with the class.

2. *Good classroom planning and procedure is the best guarantee against classroom disorder.*

It is not surprising that almost any group of beginning

teachers usually list "discipline" as their number-one concern as they undertake their work in the classroom. How to win the respect of a group of children without having them take advantage of the situation is a common worry of a young teacher. To find the proper balance between strict formality and friendly help is indeed difficult for many young teachers.

The subject of proper classroom control finds a place in almost every undergraduate methods course. W. Scott

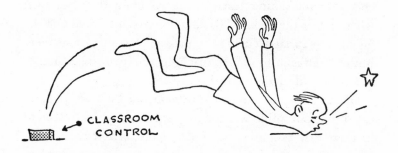

CLASSROOM
CONTROL

Smith, a New Jersey teacher-trainer of long experience, who has supervised hundreds of student teachers in New Jersey, offers thirty suggestions on the subject of classroom control. Although they were prepared with the secondary school especially in mind, a majority of these are related also to elementary school teaching.

1. Expect all pupils to report to class for the purpose of learning.

2. If a pupil fails to measure up to this expectation, let him know that you are disappointed in having your confidence abused.

3. Arrange pupils in the best manner for continuing the work at hand without interruption.

4. Adjust the physical conditions of the room so that each pupil is comfortable.

5. Learn the name of each pupil and other facts about him as soon as possible.

6. Begin work promptly so that the pupils appreciate the fact that they are there for business.

7. Plan your work carefully, and then work your plan. This includes aims, assignments, motivation, and adjusting materials to different levels of ability.

8. Plan work so that a maximum of pupil activity will result. Keep them all engaged.

9. Give pupils as much responsiblity as they can bear. Make them feel that class work is a cooperative affair.

10. Find ways of praising pupils. An ounce of praise is worth ten pounds of blame.

11. Be human. Develop a sense of humor. If the laugh is on you, grin.

12. Develop the idea that interests of the group must be respected.

13. When it is necessary to discipline a pupil, do it in private conference. Don't make an example of a child before the group.

14. When it is necessary to place the blame for some act in which two or more are involved, interview each one separately.

15. Appeal to the better side of each pupil. Prohibitive measures should be the last resort. Improvement will be made when desirable changes occur in the pupil.

16. Just before he leaves the room, make the pupil feel that his punishment is just.

17. When considering a case, imagine that it is to be tried before a jury. How would they decide it?

18. Handle all cases of discipline that you can. When necessary, send the pupil to the principals' office or get in touch with the home if that procedure is approved.

19. As soon as the pupil's punishment is over, show him that no malice is held.

20. Your job is to develop character; you are not a policeman.

21. Don't discipline any pupil while you are angry. Dispose of the case through reason and common sense.

22. Don't attempt to discipline an entire class for the misdeeds of one or a few.

23. Don't mix subject ratings with discipline.

24. Don't shout at pupils. Keep your voice low.

25. Don't let pupils know that you are annoyed by trivial acts.

26. Don't assign extra work as punishment so that the pupils learn to despise the subject.

27. Don't attempt to teach while there is disorder.

28. Don't threaten and forget to carry out the threats.

29. Don't waste too much time on discipline.

30. Don't lose too much sleep. Poor physical condition is often responsible for discipline problems.

Throughout Dr. Smith's suggestions, one notes the emphasis upon pupil motivation through meaningful work, upon good classroom planning and procedure as the best guarantee against classroom disorder. No teacher is going to find a set of readymade answers to his classroom problems, but he can find in the experiences of successful teachers the basic ingredient of classroom control—the assurance that *an ounce of prevention is worth a pound of cure.*

A classroom is a fine example of what America asks and offers in group living. The classroom that reflects cooperative effort, with full respect for the rights and responsibilities of all the members there, is one in which effort and undertaking are in the limelight and in which there is a minimum of those elements that bring the problem of control to the front. Out of respect for children, adequate planning, ample materials, ample things to be done in the classroom, a pleasing teacher personality, a democratic approach, and similar good pedagogical qualities come good classrooms. Children sense early whether a teacher likes her work and is happy in it.

Knowing the Pupils

The day has passed when we could dismiss classroom ineffectiveness on the grounds that there are too many problem children or that there are too many poor students. That there is a difference in behavior and ability among the classes in a school cannot be denied. However, the school's responsibility is to all the children. When there is this noticeable variation among class groups, a wise administrator will assign the inexperienced teacher to the class that presents no unusual problem.

In most school systems there are available for most classes and for most of the children in these classes recorded data such as cumulative record folders, health cards, standardized test scores, and confidential statements of teachers and others. In themselves these mean little to a teacher with a new class; they take on their true significance only as the teacher becomes better acquainted with the children through her own observation of their work, behavior, and characteristics. A knowledge of the out-of-school life of a child and contacts with his parents enable a teacher to use more intelligently the cumulative data that has been recorded by the school.

Although not disparaging the earnestness of educators in the scientific study of children, the writer would suggest to the new teacher that the best promise of true understanding and appreciation of her children rests with her own carefully planned relationships with them in the

classroom and around the school. The scientific movement in education, which has brought with it standardized tests, is still so relatively young that a large percentage of experienced teachers do not interpret or use effectively the scores that are made available to them. To interpret properly such data is at times almost as difficult for the teacher as to interpret directly the behavior of a child in the classroom.

For instance, the discovery of a fifth-grade reading level in a ninth-grade class, or an intelligence quotient of 155 in a fifth-grade class, still leaves the teacher with a heavy responsibility for interpretation of the data at hand. The effectiveness of such interpretation can be judged best by the alteration of teaching procedures as a result of this knowledge gained from records. As treated at length in other sections of this book, the teacher should expect wide differences in ability and behavior tendencies among the members of any class and be hesitant to throw up her hands at abilities at either extreme.

3. *The importance of the first year of teaching is overshadowed only by the importance of the first few days of that year.*

Perhaps a noticeable percentage of the teachers who fail at the job fail to get their feet on firm pedagogical ground in the first few weeks of their experience. There are no substitutes for the following procedures:

1. Plan in detail the work of the first few days, if possible with the help of principal, supervisor, or experienced teacher.

2. Understand the general school regulations before opening day, so that there'll be no undue confusion concerning routine in the classroom.

3. Establish an orderliness in the classroom the opening week that will give the pupils security without the feeling of oppression.

4. Secure the ideas and help of experienced colleagues without revealing utter dependence upon them.

5. Have at hand the books, materials, and equipment essential to carry out the plans outlined for the first few days.

6. Decorate the room prior to the opening day, so that it will give the pupils a feeling of something worth-while going on or to be done there.

These six steps should enable a new teacher to enter the first day's classroom with a feeling of security that can come only from knowing what it's all about. In contrast, imagine the handicap faced by the teacher whose first-day situation includes one or more of these situations: a completely bare room, with nothing on the boards; the lack of a piece of chalk when something has to be written on the board; a difference of opinion between teacher and pupils concerning the first day's schedule of periods; the necessity of sending some children out in search of books; or the attempt to record attendance with no knowledge of the registry system. So much of the success of teaching is nothing more than logical preparation for each day's situations.

The Orientation of New Teachers

School officials are just as eager for new teachers to get the proper start as are the teachers themselves. The conference that the superintendent used to have with the beginner, just before the opening day of school, in many school systems has now blossomed into a planned program of orientation activities. Among the procedures and materials more commonly found in orientation programs are these:

1. A preliminary meeting of all new teachers with supervisors and administrators to review matters of more urgent concern.

2. A preliminary faculty meeting in the school to introduce new members to the faculty and to opening-day routine.

3. A check-list of opening-day reports and procedures.

4. The assignment of an experienced teacher as a counselor for a new teacher.

5. A handbook of school regulations and procedures.

6. A principal's conference with the beginner.

7. Demonstrations of the use of the class register and other reports dealing with such routines as attendance taking.

Orientation courses. Some of the larger cities follow the practice of offering a semester's orientation course and requiring the attendance of all teachers new to the system. Such courses meet after school, every week or two, and are directed toward a better understanding of the system as a whole, with special emphasis upon the department in question. Supervisory and administrative personnel with whom the teacher will in time have contact appear before the group to explain the general features of their office or their work.

In San Francisco, where about a hundred and fifty new elementary teachers are added to the staff each fall, this course is provided by the Elementary School Department and led by the three general supervisors. Such special fields as art, music, and physical education are each given a meeting at which their special supervisors appear. At one meeting the group is taken on a tour through the workrooms of the Audio-Visual Aids Bureau and the Teachers' Professional Library, to give the beginners a chance to become acquainted with the services of those divisions of the system. The directors of the personnel and the salary adjustment offices talk at one meeting on the subject of the teachers' contractual status, the features of the salary schedule, and similar matters of welfare.

THE SUPERVISION OF TEACHERS

4. *Every teacher deserves adequate supervision.*

5. *Supervision is something to be sought rather than something to be feared by a new teacher.*

The teacher may have little if any control over the type of supervision that she will receive on the job, but she deserves the best of it and should do everything possible to encourage those responsible to visit her classroom. By no means should she fear such supervision.

The supervison of a new teacher has behind it two functions: (1) that of improving the education of children by helping the teacher to improve her instructional practices; and (2) that of determining if the educational welfare of the children is being handled adequately by the teacher. In other words, a program of supervision, just as anything else in the organization of things, has its being in the welfare of the pupils. Teachers are to be helped through supervision, but for the ultimate purpose of helping children to learn.

In the second of the two functions of supervision listed above rests a responsibility of administration to judge the effectiveness of a teacher in a classroom situation. It is a responsibility that school administration cannot shirk. This responsibility is a result of the fact that the public invests in an educational program and, through their school trustees, the board of education, they hold the administration responsible for the return upon that investment.

Rating Scales. In the past quarter of a century we have written much about democratic school administration, about raising the level of democratic cooperation between teachers and those responsible for supervision. In the discussion of ways to accomplish these desired relationships

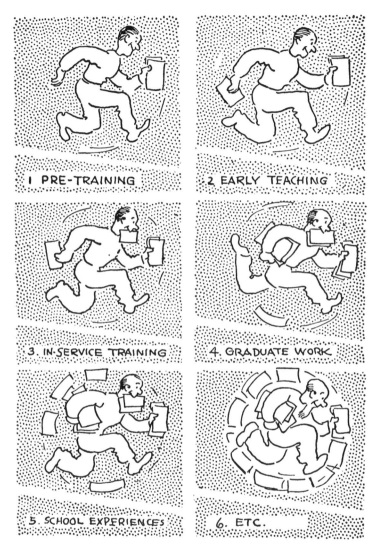

1 PRE-TRAINING

2 EARLY TEACHING

3. IN-SERVICE TRAINING

4. GRADUATE WORK

5. SCHOOL EXPERIENCES

6. ETC.

A GOOD TEACHER JUST KEEPS SNOW-BALLING ALONG

of mutual respect there has been issued an attack upon any attempt to rate the teacher by means of a system of reports. Those who attack rating have pointed out that it is difficult for administrators and supervisors to set down with any degree of objectivity a rating of a teacher's classroom work and that to attempt to do so violates the principles of good human relations.

But the fact remains that school administration cannot shirk its responsibility for efficient teaching and effective classroom instruction, detest as it may the task of having to say at the end of the year, "This teacher cannot meet the standards of instruction that our community has set up for our schools." Since this obligation of judging teaching effectiveness rests with every school superintendent's office, and since the effectiveness of a teacher's work is best determined by those who go in and out of that classroom as administrators and supervisors, it seems natural that efficiency rating blanks are used as instruments in a conscientious attempt to do the job in a fair manner. Where such rating blanks are used the administration might well be following such principles as these:

1. No rating of a teacher should be made without being discussed point by point with the teacher in a conference.

2. Ratings should represent adequate supervision and observation of the teacher in the classroom and in other situations where the teacher's work with children is being judged.

3. The rating sheet itself should be constructed in a way to give helpful suggestions to the teacher.

4. The new teacher should be given a copy of the sheet upon entrance to the school system.

5. No rating given a teacher should come as a shock,

for the act of recording the teacher's effectiveness should be one of the later steps in a series of relationships between supervisor and teacher, including an adequate number of classroom visits and conferences.

In some city and county school systems the responsibility for making out teachers' ratings rests with the principals and not with the supervisors. This reflects a common theory of American school operation that principals are line officers with administrative responsibilities but supervisors are staff officers with no administrative responsibility except that delegated to them from time to time by the superintendent. Even though a supervisor may not fill out a rating sheet for a teacher, it is common practice for the supervisor's judgment to carry weight in the superintendent's study of the case of a teacher who has received an inefficient rating.

An Example of a Rating Sheet. The example of a teacher's efficiency report that follows reveals the popular attempt to point the practice of rating toward improvement of teaching. It is to be noted that all the points on which the teacher is rated are stated in terms of good standards of teaching. The form from which this scale was taken included other features besides this rating.

1. Personal Characteristics	Outstanding	Satisfactory	Unsatisfactory	Failing
	1	2	3	4

_____ Adjusts readily to new situations and tasks

_____ Appreciates supervision and guidance

_____ Cooperates well with the administration

_____ Works well with children and commands their respect

_____ Maintains pleasant and cooperative relationships with other staff members

———— Works well with, and gains the respect of, parents
———— Shows care in personal appearance
———— Displays emotional stability
———— Displays interest and enthusiasm in teaching
———— Exercises good judgment and diplomacy
———— Speaks and acts in a manner that is highly professional
———— Shows evidence of good health

2. Classroom Teaching	Outstanding	Satisfactory	Unsatisfactory	Failing
	1	2	3	4

———— Sees clearly the goals of instruction for the term
———— Plans well for each day's work
———— Reveals a good knowledge of content and methods of the particular class level
———— Reveals a good knowledge of the course of study and teaching materials
———— Has good control of the classroom situation
———— Handles effectively and efficiently the routine of classroom management
———— Respects the worth and dignity of the individual pupil
———— Provides for individual differences among pupils
———— Gives careful attention to the physical conditions and appearance of the classroom
———— Secures good results in teaching
———— Seeks improved ways of teaching

3. Out-of-classroom Work	Outstanding	Satisfactory	Unsatisfactory	Failing
	1	2	3	4

———— Helps effectively in out-of-class supervision of children, as in corridors, cafeteria, school yard, auditorium
———— Meets time schedules promptly, keeps records accurately, and files reports promptly

_____ Co-operates willingly in extra-class school and community activities

_____ Recognizes that much of teacher's clerical work must be done during non-teaching time

4. Composite Rating	Outstanding	Satisfactory	Unsatisfactory	Failing
	1	2	3	4

TOPICS FOR STUDY AND DISCUSSION

1. Make an area survey of teachers with one year's experience to determine their suggestions for succeeding in the first assignment.

2. Why does "discipline" seem to be a major problem of the beginning teacher in so many instances?

3. From Dr. Smith's list of 30 suggestions designate which apply especially to elementary teaching and which to secondary.

4. Examine as a group a variety of cumulative record cards, standardized tests, and other instruments available to teachers for knowing their pupils.

5. List the orientation services that a beginning teacher should expect in being adjusted to a new position.

6. Discuss the possible use and misuse of teachers' rating blanks.

Chapter 12

The Teacher and School Administration

1. *No teacher teaches alone.*

Even though she may teach behind closed doors or in a one-room school, no teacher teaches alone. The classroom is tied closely into a larger school organization. Somewhere in the scheme of things is an administrator—a superintendent or a principal, or both. And in a county or a large-city system there are various other staff members with supervisory responsibility.

No teacher teaches alone, for behind every classroom in America there is a school organization, and behind the organization are systems of administration and supervision. It is true that at the heart of education is the teacher with her brood gathered around her, but this learning situation is buttressed by a school organization with its detail of administrative and supervisory provisions—buttressed against inadequate school support, against inefficient teaching procedures, against public misunderstanding, and against all the other enemies of good teaching conditions. The organization behind the classroom is highly essential.

First, there is the organization of the school system into different units, the elementary school, the junior high, and the senior high school. Within each there are grade levels. Marking systems, testing programs, teachers' registers, schedules of classes and recesses, home reports, teacher rating sheets, and a hundred other practices and devices reflect the administrative structure that encompass the teacher's classroom.

2. *Instruction, the queen of education, will always be highly dependent upon her handmaidens, organization, administration, and supervision.*

The lesson planning that the teacher carries on day in and day out has its parallel in the administrative planning that goes on day in and day out in the operation of a school system, large or small.

Local School Organization

3. *Schools must be organized that they may be taught; school organization has no other justification.*

There are just as many systems of organization as there are school systems. In a small Indiana town where there is one school and all the children are taught under the same roof, there may be an organization something like this:

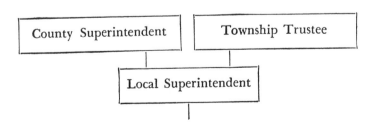

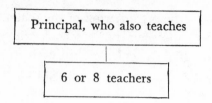

In this situation the teacher secures his position and his pay check through the township trustee, but he secures his professional leadership from a county superintendent who serves all the schools in the county. At the other extreme in the organization of schools is a large city system with its labyrinth of administrative and supervisory channels.

The teacher who enters a large school system, such as the one represented on page 255, sometimes has a little difficulty understanding his exact relationship to all of the various staff members who are connected either directly or remotely with the superintendent's office and who work between that office and the schools. Indeed, in the large city system there seems to be an endless number of workers between the teacher's classroom and the superintendent's office. There are the associate superintendent, the assistants, the co-ordinators A and B, the directors, the supervisors A and B, and others.

Needless to say, because of the complexity of functions in a system of this kind only a limited number of these staff members work directly with any one teacher at his given grade or subject level. The principal is the one to acquaint the new teacher with these staff workers, especially the ones doing direct classroom supervision, and to see that a relationship is effected promising maximum contribution to the classroom situation. The wise superintendent works diligently at the task of using his staff of

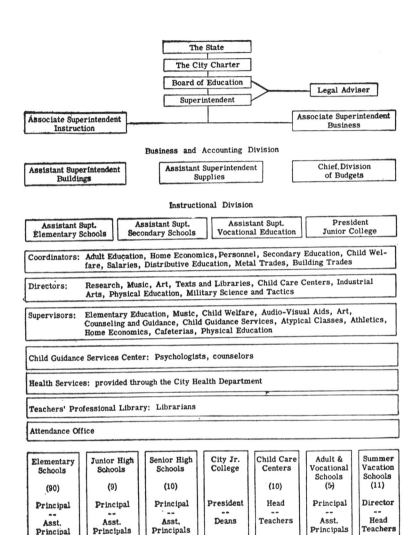

The State

The City Charter

Board of Education

Superintendent — Legal Adviser

Associate Superintendent
Instruction

Associate Superintendent
Business

Business and Accounting Division

Assistant Superintendent
Buildings

Assistant Superintendent
Supplies

Chief, Division
of Budgets

Instructional Division

Assistant Supt.
Elementary Schools

Assistant Supt.
Secondary Schools

Assistant Supt.
Vocational Education

President
Junior College

Coordinators: Adult Education, Home Economics, Personnel, Secondary Education, Child Welfare, Salaries, Distributive Education, Metal Trades, Building Trades

Directors: Research, Music, Art, Texts and Libraries, Child Care Centers, Industrial Arts, Physical Education, Military Science and Tactics

Supervisors: Elementary Education, Music, Child Welfare, Audio-Visual Aids, Art, Counseling and Guidance, Child Guidance Services, Atypical Classes, Athletics, Home Economics, Cafeterias, Physical Education

Child Guidance Services Center: Psychologists, counselors

Health Services: provided through the City Health Department

Teachers' Professional Library: Librarians

Attendance Office

Elementary Schools (90)	Junior High Schools (9)	Senior High Schools (10)	City Jr. College	Child Care Centers (10)	Adult & Vocational Schools (5)	Summer Vacation Schools (11)
Principal -- Asst. Principal -- Teachers	Principal -- Asst. Principals -- Counselors -- Teachers	Principal -- Asst. Principals -- Counselors -- Teachers	President -- Deans -- Teachers	Head -- Teachers --	Principal -- Asst. Principals -- Teachers	Director -- Head Teachers -- Teachers

assistants to tie the schools closely to the central office, for teacher loyalty and morale is dependent upon a feeling of belonging to a unified enterprise. The teacher in the city school has to exert more effort himself to secure this feeling than does the small town teacher who every day sees everyone else in his school system, including the superintendent, the principal, all the other teachers, and usually the trustee.

THE JUSTIFICATION OF ADMINISTRATION

4. *School organization and administration have but one justification—the education of children.*

Those of us who carry administrative responsibilities need to pause in our duties now and then just long enough to recall that school organization and administration are not ends but means. They have but one justification, the better education of children.

When administration carries the perfection of the organization of the school to an extreme, school operation can reach a stage of efficiency that hinders education. For instance, the high-school principal may not permit anybody to change his program after the first month of school, it being disconcerting to think of breaking the smoothly running schedule of classes.

Or the principal may place teacher monitors at all doors and in the halls rather than let student leaders assume such duties, the smooth operation of the school being better assured with the teachers on such posts.

Or an elementary-school teacher may find herself working out a daily lesson plan as an end in itself. A lesson plan, regardless of how well organized, means little unless it is carried over into the actual activities of children in the classroom.

On the other hand, the school could place education ahead of organization. A pupil might change his program of classes as late as the middle of the term if such change assures a more promising school adjustment for him. And students might handle the traffic posts and the direction of study halls because such activities are opportunities for education.

The elementary-school teacher may organize her class into three groups to facilitate instruction and learning, but she will not hesitate to change her organization at any time that another seems to suit the situation better. Two groups, or one group with special attention to a few individuals, may invite her attention at the middle of the term.

The marking system, as commonly used in our schools, must likewise be listed on the organization side of the ledger rather than on the side of instruction. It is merely a system of reporting progress and should be judged on that basis alone.

There is nothing sacred about any of our techniques of organization and administration. They are tested by the results in learning. We should accept them always as flexible procedures subject to change when instructional results seem to invite such change.

5. *The more we look upon each school level as preparation for the one ahead, the greater will be the gaps between them.*

Early this century the junior high school was created to bridge the gap between the 8-year elementary school and the 4-year high school. In spite of the fine work that has been accomplished by many junior high schools, in other instances two gaps have been created, one between the 6-year elementary school and the 3-year junior high school, and the other between the junior high school and the 3-year senior high school.

The success of any system of school organization, be it the 8-4, the 6-3-3, the 6-6, the 6-4-4, or the what-not, depends upon the system's being built from the bottom up, rather than from the top down.

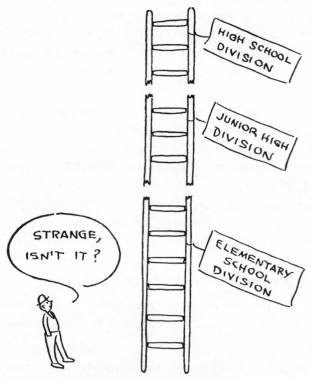

THE BREAKS OF THE GAME

The top-down complex causes a school to follow certain curriculum practices that are dictated by the expectations of the school above. The inability of pupils to carry through such a program or their disinterest in doing so leaves a gap between that school level and the one above. With the framework of the American high school—with its academic program built down from the college, with the typical junior high program built down from the high school, and with the elementary school program built up from the bottom—it is no wonder that there have been gaps.

Let the elementary school take the child as he is when he enters the kindergarten and build each new year's work for him in accordance with the experiences, abilities, needs, and interests that he brings out of the previous year. Then let the junior high take him as he is when he enters and build each new year's work for him in accordance with the experiences, abilities, needs, and interests that he brings out of the previous year. Let the senior high school follow the same practice. And let each college select those that it wishes according to its traditions, and do the same. With this program there will be no so-called gaps.

6. *It's not the system of organization, it's what the teacher does with the group of pupils in front of him that counts.*

Providing a proper program of education is something much more intricate than organizing. American educators are the finest organizers afoot. Even American business and industry must take off their hats to school organization. But we must not mistake the limitations of organization.

Every so often in the organization of schools somebody has proposed a new scheme for grouping the various grades of the school system. At first it was the 8-4 and the 7-4 plans. Then it was the 6-3-3 and the 6-6. Then a handful of schools traipsed after the pied piper with the 6-4-4 tune.

There's little reason to get excited about the divisions we make in our educational ladder from kindergarten through the fourteenth grade. It's not the organization that counts, but what the teacher does with the group of pupils in front of him, how he does it, plus what administrative leadership does to help him to do a better job with that group of pupils.

The Teacher's Attitude about Organization

7. The teacher's obligation is to the child at hand not to the teacher at the next higher grade level.

The expectations of the teacher at the seventh-grade level should not set the curriculum for the teacher at the sixth, nor should the expectations of the sixth-grade teacher set the curriculum for the teacher of the fifth grade.

The expectations of the high school should not set the curriculum of the junior high school, nor should the expectations of the junior high school set the curriculum of the elementary school.

If each teacher is true to the child at hand, his nature and his needs, there need be no concern about the teacher at the next grade level or the possible adjustment of the child at that level.

8. *The school's obligation is to the pupil at hand not to the next higher educational institution.*

Just as the teacher's obligation is to the pupil in his class and not to the teacher at the next grade level, so is the school's obligation to the pupil and not to the next higher educational institution.

The elementary school takes its being and meaning from the pupil that it is serving. If it is true to that pupil's abilities and needs, the high school can ask no more.

The high school takes its being and meaning from the pupil that it is serving. If it is true to that pupil's abilities and needs, the college can ask no more.

9. *Teachers at any school level need to accept graciously all the pupils that enter from the school below.*

Our struggling profession harbors too many teachers who feel sorry for themselves every time they look at their new classes. They blame the school below as if to say, "Look what somebody did to me!" These teachers unprofessionally speak of good classes and poor classes.

If our trade ever achieves the full stature of a profession, teachers must extend their sympathy to their pupils rather than retain it for themselves. As long as we are shocked at the limitations of human nature and at the big gap between human nature and our own pedagogical ideals, we are indeed limited in attempting to fit the school to the pupil.

If there is one group of workers in the world who through training and experience should take a philo-

sophical and sympathetic attitude toward the variegations of mankind it is the teaching group. It is easy to understand why the banker or the storekeeper will speak out, "You haven't taught them arithmetic." For he is seeking perfection in abilities that will bring returns to himself. It is easy to understand why the editor or the office manager will say, "You haven't taught them to write." For his is a business enterprise placing monetary value upon that specific ability.

But that teachers at seventh or tenth grade level can work themselves up over the fact that all students can't reach a given standard in using numbers or in distinguishing between declarative, interrogative, and exclamatory sentences is not justifiable. A normal progression through school is implied by the graded system, and the gracious acceptance of each new class by the teacher is the least he can do to recognize and help the normal development of children who are growing up as they are moving up through the grades of the school.

INSTRUCTIONAL STANDARDS

10. *Instructional standards are false unless they are set in accordance with the natures of those to be served.*

With the organization of school systems into units and levels of instruction, into classes and groupings within classes, there come ideals of instruction and standards. Teachers and layman alike speak of lowering and raising standards.

We who have acted as school administrators have seen junior and senior high school youth persecuted day after day because of their shortcomings in the use of their native language and their handicaps in getting ideas from the printed page. And it was all glossed over as the school's respect for standards.

Respect for human nature comes first, and standards are false unless they are set in accordance with the natures of those to be served. At times, junior and senior high school

gym teachers have developed a rating system that penalized the physically immature who could not climb the rope, chin the bar, or run the obstacle course as effectively as their mates. In accepting graciously those who come up from the school below, the teacher refrains from judging and thus classifying the pupils on the basis of scholastic aptitude.

Democracy proposes to enable all to rise to their full stature and to make the most of their talents, abundant or meager, for the good of themselves and their society. In following this democratic ideal, the good teacher sets the standards of his class in true relationship to the unique natures of those to be served.

11. *A grade in a school takes its meaning or significance from the particular children in that grade. It has no significance without them.*

That the children in a grade give it meaning is well illustrated in the first grade of the school. The first grade in a school that has lowered its minimum entrance age to 5 years and 6 months calls for a program quite different from that which it offered when the minimum entrance age was 5 years and 9 months. Three months' difference in the maturity of 5 and 6 year old children is highly significant in respect to readiness for formal school work such as reading.

In a large school system with the same minimum entrance age throughout the city, the first grade in a well-to-do residential section is quite different from the first grade in an impoverished section of the city, where children have been deprived of enriched pre-school experiences in their homes and neighborhoods.

Although the American public has come to think of the first grade as the reading grade, the profession is increasingly becoming aware of the fact that both the work and the expectancy must be true to the maturity of the children at hand, and that readiness for first grade does not necessarily mean readiness for reading.

To give significance to the first grade without considering the particular children being served will result in heavy
failures. To let the grade take its significance from the
group at hand means a natural advancement through the
grade, experiences being provided in accordance with the
maturity of the children.

That failure at this beginning step of the American
school ladder results in approximately 20 per cent mor-
tality each year is a fact that reflects the schools' failure
to permit the meaning of the grade to spring from the
maturity of the children.

12. *Education is a matter of time and place.*

As to place—in a large city system the educational needs
of children in one section may vary greatly from those of
the same age in another. Second-grade expectations in
reading in one section may be similar to first-grade expectations in another. The curriculum in the high school
that is on the edge of town, drawing from an agricultural
area just outside, should vary greatly from the curriculum
of the high school in the heart of the industrial section
and from the curriculum of the school in the residential
section where so many are bound for college.

As to time—the program of the school in wartime
must be noticeably different from that of the same school
a few years later in time of peace. The school that reflects
the life of the community will change with the times.

A static curriculum is followed and the distinctions of
changing times and those of varying places are ignored
only when those who determine school policy place their
faith in some misconception of education such as the theory
of mental discipline.

Within a single school itself education must vary greatly from one child to another, and within a single classroom the good teacher knows that there are as many "places" as there are children. Likewise, the good teacher varies his program from time to time, so that over a period of two years the work in the same grade or the same subject varies noticeably.

13. *Offering every child the chance to attend a free public school does not in itself mean equal educational opportunity.*

Education for all American children is not the same as education *fitted* to all American children. The high school that offers a limited curriculum, suitable for only a portion of youth, is not providing education for all the youth of that community. The school whose teachers restrict their interest and kindliness to only the more scholastically promising is restricting its program to only a portion of the community's children.

Good teachers in either an elementary or a high school classroom see pupil needs not by whole-class groups, but by individual or small-group needs. Individualizing instruction, compromising between pedagogical ideals and human possibilities, placing the child before the subject— these and similar teaching techniques assure a school fitted to all the children of all the people.

The fifth-grade requirement that represents a standard out of line with the learning possibilities of some of the group results in a selective school. The play of Shakespeare that must be mastered by all tenth-grade English pupils results in a selective school.

Offering a program of public education to all the children is an educational challenge that has never been fully met in America. The process of fitting is still being perfected.

This process of fitting, as carried forward on the local level, represents administrative supervision and leadership.

SUPERVISION AND MEASUREMENT

14. *The most effective supervision is that which focuses attention upon the improvement of the learning situation rather than on the improvement of the individual teacher.*

Good teaching calls for good teachers, and this calls for supervisory leadership. However, it does not necessarily follow that the improvement of teachers in service will be best accomplished through a program emphasizing their weaknesses.

Supervisors, administrators, and teachers have one thing in common—the growth and development of children. This being true, the common focus of attention should be upon the learning situation. However, some school systems seem to focus attention upon the pattern for administration.

When the pattern of administration is emphasized, teachers are made to feel that they are responsible to supervisors and administrators rather than to children and learning. There is a great emphasis upon authority and lines of operation. Levels of operation are quite apparent, with teachers on the lower, principals on one just above, and top administrators on the top level of operation. Under this plan of operation, orders and directions from above take on such significance that the teacher's loyalty to a pattern of operation takes precedence over her loyalty to child growth and development.

On the other hand, in the school system in which the learning situation is the common center of attention, supervisory officers and teachers work together on common instructional problems. Starting with a mutual recogni-

tion of instructional weaknesses, they develop new classroom materials, experiment with new methods, and otherwise co-operate in improving the learning situation. There isn't time to bother about who is in authority, who is weak, and who has the ideas to be followed. Just as children will grow through the enriched program developed for them, so the participating teachers and supervisors are growing through the planning of that program.

15. *Test scores are to be used, not misused.*

The scientific movement in education, in spite of its

apparent limitations, has produced standardized tests that help teachers to see better the abilities, possibilities, and limitations of their students. But the score from such a test in the hands of a misguided teacher can bring harm instead of good to the student in question. For instance, once upon a time there was a geometry teacher who could not determine the first set of marks to be taken home by her students, until she had gone to their permanent records in the office to see what scores they had made on the diagnostic mathematics test given them at the time they entered high school.

You would use a low mathematics score or a low reading score not as evidence that you as a teacher are helpless in the case, but rather, as an indication of the nature of the work by which the student might profit. Just as soon as you discover that one student in your ninth grade class reads on the level of the average sixth-grader and another on the level of the average twelfth-grader, the whole matter of differentiated teaching materials and expectations begins wigwagging for your attention.

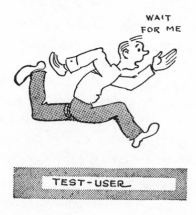

Once they are determined, test scores are not to be used as brands on children to enable all teachers coming their way thereafter to detect the portion of the herd worth fattening from the portion that should be shipped back to the public just as soon as possible. The purposes to which test scores are put should always be constructive, constructive for the children to whom those scores belong.

16. *It is much simpler to give a standardized test than it is to use the scores.*

Test-makers and test-givers are still far ahead of test-users in the American educational scene. Filing cabinets in school offices all over the land are bulging with prognostic, diagnostic, achievement, aptitude, intelligence, reading, and miscellaneous test scores. Students come and students go but test scores are filed forever.

Tests can be given by the hundreds, but once secured each score must be treated individually if it is to bring benefit to the student in question. A testing program means little in itself. It means something only if under-

TEST-GIVER   TEST-MAKER

standing counselors, administrators, and teachers use the scores from day to day in growth relationships with students.

The test director has a right to expect teachers to use test results. The teacher has a right to proper directions in the use of these results. And the student has a right to better learning conditions because of all this. Wherever test-giving is too far ahead of test-using, the giving should be held up until the using catches up.

Topics for Study and Discussion

1. The chapter carries charts of a large and a small school system. Chart the organization of a school system of which you have common knowledge.

2. What may prevent a school from following the idea that a school system needs to be built from the lower grades up, rather than from the college down?

3. To what extent do we still find in American schools violation of principle 9 of this chapter?

4. Most school systems use age-grade progress charts. Bring some of these to the group meeting to discuss their nature, purpose, and use.

5. Describe *equality of educational opportunity* as you understand the concept.

6. What does a beginning teacher need to know about test construction? How does this vary with grade level and subject to be taught?

Chapter 13

Professional Relationships

TEACHING IS A MATTER OF HUMAN RELATIONSHIPS, FOR THE
teacher is always dealing with people. Only when he with-
draws to prepare plans for the next day's classroom or to
mark a few papers or score some tests is he really practicing
his trade alone.

From the first day on the job he is well aware that *the
main ingredient of the classroom is children.* When he
frees himself from the pupils at the noon hour to grab a
bite of lunch, he is in the presence of administrators and
other teachers, with whom he usually talks shop across
the table. This tendency to exchange notes with other
teachers during the lunch hour reflects the limited amount
of time that teachers have away from their own classrooms
during the school day to work and plan together.

After school there are parents to meet, sometimes individually and at times in groups, such as those assembled
for a meeting of the Parent-Teacher Association. In his
out-of-school life he can hardly leave his professional
affairs behind. Instead, it is quite natural for him to talk
shop with the people who make up his social and personal-
business contacts. Next to the weather, there is no general

topic of conversation so popular in the typical American community as schools. It reflects the great investment that America has made in a system of public education and the public interest and faith in what schools can do.

When an article dealing with schools appears in a popular magazine, a teacher's reaction is bound to be solicited by his butcher, his baker, or his candlestick maker. As one on the inside of the profession, the teacher finds himself in the midst of the community concern about schools, and he cannot escape this professional role as the community shows interest in such matters as:

1. The election of new school board members.

2. The presentation to the voters of a proposed bond issue for new school buildings.

3. The possibility of the local high school basketball team winning the state tournament.

4. The agitation in the state legislature for a teachers' loyalty oath.

5. A criticism of the program of the local schools made by a prominent citizen.

6. The question of the need for a new school building.

7. The announcement of a pronounced change in the curriculum of the schools.

It has long been established that success in teaching means a lot more than success in taking courses in education.

1. *Success in teaching reflects success in working with people.*

It is apparent that the person who doesn't enjoy having people around has no business entering this profession. It first means enjoyment in being with children, but the teacher's successful relationships cannot be limited to those with pupils alone. Effective ways of working with principals, other teachers, supervisors, parents, and laymen interested in education are essential to a successful teaching career.

Most of the chapters of this book have emphasized the importance of classroom performance, and there is no intention now to minimize the significance of that work. This chapter represents an attempt to show that the teaching role calls for even more than good classroom performance.

RELATIONSHIPS WITH PARENTS

Some years back, a great deal was written about a school's public relations program; these writings placed the major responsibility for good public relations with the superintendent's office and placed the greatest faith in newspaper stories, radio programs, and talks before public groups. At that time the theory was that of "selling the schools to the public" through a program of publicity developed specifically for the purpose. Today the pendulum has swung in the opposite direction. The value of informing the public through radio, press, television, and assembly is fully appreciated, but it is realized that such a program is one of informing, not selling, and that it merely supplements the main oracle, which is the school itself.

2. *The work of the teacher is the most effective instrument that any school has for establishing public understanding of and confidence in the schools.*

Every teacher has a direct connection with the homes represented by the children in his classroom. These lines of communication, and consequently lines of interpretation or misinterpretation, are kept open through the home report cards, the teacher's contacts with parents, and the stories of school taken home by the children. These channels are not to be taken lightly. A fifth-grade teacher blamed her class severely for their behavior and attitudes toward work, and on the home report cards marked fully a third of the group down in citizenship. The blame that she tried to pass on to the homes came back like a boomerang in the form of disgruntled children and parents. The parents wanted to know exactly who was to blame for the lack of success in that classroom.

3. *The strongest thing that can be said for a school is the good word that a child takes home about it, and the worst thing is the criticism that he takes home.*

The work of the teacher in effecting good school-home relationships is of two types: (1) good classroom instruction and (2) pleasant and helpful contacts with parents. Even the young children soon come to appreciate if their classroom is an effective unit of operation.

Some time ago the writer visited the second-grade classroom of a beginning teacher; this room gave the impression of a pen full of young chicks running aimlessly here and there. The lack of order reflected lack of purpose on the part of both pupils and teacher. The disorderly arrangement of the room and the poor housekeeping must have had their effect upon those seven-year-old children. The whole thing promised poor home reactions to the work of the school. In contrast to this, both the stability and the richness of experience that were reflected in the rooms on either side must have resulted in close bonds between school and home.

This is not to say that the teacher's first task is to please parents. Rather, her task is to set up the proper working conditions in the room to assure maximum growth and learning for the children. Which is to say that although

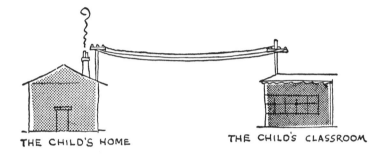

THE CHILD'S HOME   THE CHILD'S CLASSROOM

a classroom teacher is the school's best public relations agent, he doesn't necessarily think about or work at that task directly. His good job in the classroom speaks for itself.

Parents in Education. The organization of public education, as outlined in Chapters 4 and 12, is one that represents a balance between professional workers and laymen. Through the state legislature, the state board of education, and the local board of education, the citizens assume official duties in helping to determine and control school programs. It is estimated that the number of school board members, commissioners, and similar trustees in American public education exceeds 400,000, which means that for every two or three teachers there is one citizen working actively in school organization. Behind all of this more formal school machinery are the hundreds of thousands of parents who show their interest through membership in parent groups such as the Parent-Teacher Association.

The Parent-Teacher Association. There is no more potent force for the defense of progress in American education and for its further advancement than the Parent-Teacher Association. Nationally, the organization is known as the National Congress of Parents and Teachers. It has approximately 6 million members. Believing in education for all the children of all the people, since its origin the Association has worked on the principle that all the people have a vital concern in education and the schools and should show it openly. The organization takes an active part in school elections and school board appointments. It does this in a non-political manner, setting standards for school board membership and studying the qualifications of candidates, but not endorsing candidates as Parent-Teacher Association or officer of such. In a few cities in which school board members are appointed by the mayor, the PTA is still struggling to have the city hall follow a list of standards to guide the selection of board members. In general, the local associations in the past have been interested in such projects as these:

1. Helping to secure qualified school board members.

2. Supporting adequate school revenue programs rather than buying things for the local school.

3. Developing projects for the health of children.

4. Studying the work of the schools, but not interfering with their professional direction.

5. Advancing provisions for equal educational opportunities for all children.

6. Seeking to secure good working conditions such as small classes in a school.

7. Encouraging the policy of a principal over every school.

8. Defending teacher salaries as the budget item of greatest importance next to that of fixed charges.

9. Encouraging an enriched curriculum.

10. Studying school finance.

11. Extending better working relationships between home and school; bringing teachers and parents together.

12. Sponsoring bills before legislative bodies that promote the welfare of child, home, and school.

4. *The success of a Parent-Teacher Association is as dependent upon the teacher's participation as upon the parent's.*

The list of activities just cited is typical of the work of Parent-Teacher Associations. A comprehensive list of such activities would be a book in itself. Those listed are sufficient to show that the work of the Association is dependent upon the teacher's participation as well as the parent's. The national by-laws point out the essential place of the teacher in this movement for better schools. Perhaps the close home-school cooperation that the school seeks for each teacher's classroom is exemplified on the broad scale by the work of the Parent-Teacher Association. It seeks to join the parents as a group in a program of study and action.

In some schools the active participation of the teachers has never been fully achieved. This is often due to a schedule of meetings during school hours, which denies the teacher the opportunity to attend. Many schools have overcome this difficulty by scheduling at least every other meeting as an evening meeting. This plan likewise makes it possible for fathers to participate.

In Highland Park, Illinois, the author once inaugurated the plan of a shortened schedule of classes on the days of the monthly Parent-Teacher meetings, thus assuring the Association the participation of the teachers in its afternoon meetings.

At times the parents in a local Parent-Teacher unit, in their eagerness, tend to forget the possibility of including the teachers as an effective element in the organization.

5. *America's public schools are founded upon the intense interest of parents in their children.*

It takes the young teacher some time to appreciate the parent's place in the educational scheme of things. If at times the parent's interest in the child's school situation appears somewhat selfish, it can be accepted as being as natural as the rearing of children. Rather than to attempt to draw a line between selfish interest and intense interest on a parent's part, it is better to sum up all parent interest as a force that serves as a cornerstone of public education. Without this keen attention that parents give to the work and the adjustment of their children in school, the schools would be cut off from both present purpose and future promise.

Perhaps in most schools the kindergarten and first-grade teachers see a greater percentage of the parents of their pupils than the teachers of other grade levels. This represents the concern of parents for the safety and welfare of the very young child who enters school. It likewise represents the concern of the parent when sending the child to school for the first time. It is a period of adjustment for the mother as well as the child. It is at these early grade levels that the school needs to work hard at the job of making parents realize that they are expected to maintain this close interest in school throughout the remaining years of the child's attendance.

6. *The interest of parents in the work of the school needs to be encouraged by all teachers.*

It is the individual teacher who has the greatest opportunity to exert the influence necessary to maintain this early interest of the parent. There is nothing secret about the formula for this; it is merely a matter of capitalizing upon the normal concern of a parent for the child and revealing the school's same close interest in this child's welfare. Such a formula suggests simple but effective procedures such as these:

1. The teacher works at the job of becoming a good host for his classroom. He reveals friendliness to parents upon all occasions. Parents soon know whether or not they are welcome in a classroom or a school.

2. The teacher invites parents individually or in groups to school to observe the work of the classroom. With experience comes a general knowledge of the common concerns of parents about school and school procedures. Many primary teachers anticipate the concern that a mother reveals in the beginning reading program and respect this interest by setting up classroom demonstrations of the steps in reading instruction.

Many high schools appreciate the fact that the parents of the pupils in the beginning class want to know about the work of the school but are reluctant to come in alone. Here again, whole-school open house programs and visiting days for the individual classrooms can do much to capitalize upon the normal interest of parents in their children.

3. The teacher develops an appreciation of the significance of the work that a child carries home from school. Papers collected over a period of time, arranged neatly in a folder, accompanied by a note from the teacher, can mean a lot to a parent in understanding the worth of the school program. The importance of the work that pupils do under teachers' direction, at high school as well as elementary level, justifies care in the arrangement of such work for parents' examination.

4. The school, through its principal and teachers, should establish with the home the feeling that any parental concern about the child's adjustment in the school can be taken up with teacher or principal without loss of position for the child. In his administrative experience in a number of states and school systems, the author has come to realize that a noticeable fraction of the parents of school children are reluctant to approach the school with their problems for fear "it will be taken out on the child." This feeling may represent a carry-over from the days when school procedure was not to be questioned by home and when parents were not expected to come around the school unless sent for by the authorities. Regardless of its origin, school people need to take steps to see that this has no justification today.

7. *The school that operates without an active interest of parents is limited in its educational effectiveness.*

The close relationship of home and school is commonly accepted today in school operation, so much so that the absence of an active interest of parents in a school suggests a program somewhat limited in its effectiveness. The modern school cannot expect to reach its goals without the help of the school patrons.

8. *Due to the significance of proper parent-teacher relationships in the development of the child, the teacher should command the respect of the parents in dealing with the child.*

Needless to say, full respect for the school's efforts is dependent upon an adequate knowledge of those efforts. This in turn implies such parental relationships as those already discussed in this chapter. Full respect for any teacher will come with understanding of and respect for the work of that teacher. This understanding cannot be left to chance.

9. *The teacher can cement home-school relationships by the proper use of the home report card.*

Home report cards in themselves can never carry the message of the school's efforts into the homes. However, a well-prepared card, carefully used by the teacher, can do much to cement the various relationships already existing between home and school. The reporting of the teacher's judgment of the progress and the status of the child in the school is the purpose of the report card. It behooves the teacher to use the card for this purpose and to guard against injecting other motives in the use of the reporting system. In warning against the misuse of the reporting system, G. M. Wingo has made this statement:

> It should be pointed out that school marks have usually served many purposes besides reporting to

parents. They have practically always been used by some teachers for the purpose of providing rewards and punishment for doing or not doing school work. With certain kinds of children they can be very powerful in this respect. When used with finesse by a cunning teacher, school marks can be used for punishment to a degree which would make physical punishment seem mild by comparison. It is not meant to be implied that all teachers, or even very many teachers, use school marks in this way, but the possibility is always present.[1]

No doubt home report cards would never have originated had there been available to teachers frequent face-to-face contacts with the parents of their pupils. Schools are continuing to build up these personal relationships, and home reports seem to tell more in such a setting. Some schools have substituted personal letters for report cards, and others have attempted to replace cards by bringing each parent to the school at intervals for a conference with the teacher. Such substitutions for the card are few and there is every indication that report cards have been accepted as a worthy link between teacher and parent. There promises to be a continued attempt to improve these report cards.

10. *The public attitude about a school program is reflected in public school expenditures.*

The way of the schools is dependent upon the will of the people. This is just as true in a financial as in an instructional sense. A general indifference about the work of the school or a feeling that it is ineffectual is bound to

---

[1] G. M. Wingo, "Reporting to Parents in the Elementary School," *School of Education Bulletin*, University of Michigan, April, 1949, pp. 104-105.

be reflected in the inclination of the community to hold down school expenditures to a minimum. Bonds for a new school plant could hardly be floated on such a feeling of indifference about education. A better salary schedule for teachers, calling for higher school budget, can be pleaded for on the grounds of an increase in the cost of living, but it is more apt to be achieved because of an increase in the community satisfaction with the work of the school.

THE LIFE OF THE COMMUNITY

11. In personal and social relationships the teacher must maintain at all times ethical and moral standards that are socially acceptable in the school district and the school.

One who enters the service of teaching soon realizes that society entertains certain expectations of those who teach, such expectations being defined from time to time by the expression of a portion of the local citizenry. That these ideas of proper teacher's performance include out-of-school conduct as well as actual classroom outputs is not a surprise to one of many years of service. At times it is learned the hard way by the beginner.

It is not our place here to treat the merits of these public expectations of the one to whom the children of the community are entrusted for learning. It is merely to recall that the one who serves the public in the classroom of America works under somewhat different conditions from those he would encounter as a salesman of tractors, a proprietor of the corner grocery, or a secretary in a large insurance firm. Furthermore, there is no one general public code of ethics for teachers in vogue throughout the

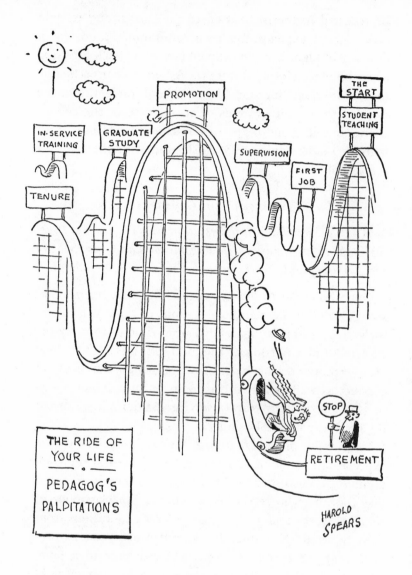

THE RIDE OF
YOUR LIFE
o
PEDAGOG'S
PALPITATIONS

HAROLD
SPEARS

country. This status of a teacher is reflected by the mores of the particular community in which he serves.

With no intention of indicating how another should govern his life, it can be said that in personal and social relationships, the teacher must maintain at all times ethical and moral standards that are socially acceptable in the particular school district. The public attitude about teachers reflects the great influence that teachers exert upon their pupils. Children's appreciation of things, whether or not of literature, music, governmental philosophy, or social customs, is greatly influenced by the attitudes of the adults in their lives—especially parents and teachers.

Harlan C. Koch, experienced teacher of teachers in the state of Michigan, has revealed his concern for those "teachers who are victims of certain frustrations which, like slow paralysis, gradually inactivate their early enthusiasm for teaching." In trying to condition teachers to certain attitudes of the public toward their work, attitudes which tend to break down a teacher's sense of self-respect, he makes this statement:

> Whether teaching is any better or any worse than other professions for the practitioners' peace of mind cannot, of course, be easily determined. All have their unique difficulties. But that amorphous creature, the Public, so often both fickle and cruel, is only an aggregate of individuals who share the attributes common to mankind. Here, perhaps, a solution of the problem can be found. Those who really believe in teaching as a call to social service will be the first to recognize that the common or garden variety of citizen also believes in it as such. Consequently, he and his fellows have established a code of conduct for those who would

teach, which easily compares with that devised for the clergy. Those who aspire to teach but cannot subscribe to this cold fact should go no further. Others who have learned it by experience and still rebel, should quit the profession. Those who remain should recognize that, generally speaking, the public estimate of any profession is roughly an accurate one. How, then, down through the years have teachers themselves contributed to the attitudes which they now lament? Are they really a "type"? Are they actually ineffectual in the give and take of everyday life? Are they too stilted and bookish?

Evidently the problem is one of public relations in the finest sense of the term. The initiative obviously rests with the teachers, and the approach is through the individual citizen. Service intelligently rendered to him, then, by cultured, human, and likeable teachers will, in the long run, win the regard which they crave. With it will also come those privileges whose denial now weighs upon the teachers' peace of mind. Full commitment, as Averill puts it, "to temperateness and inner control" is, however, a prerequisite. Vigorous resistance to any community's traditions, customs, superstitions, or beliefs about life in general, or ideas about teachers and teaching in particular, is inconsistent with this principle. It can lead only to further mental confusion. Strenuous defense of one's "rights" may indeed win a battle but lose the war. Instead, identification of one's self with social or civic groups in the community is for most people a condition for happy personal living. For the teacher, this means losing himself, or herself as the case may be, in the opportunities for helpfulness which life in the community affords. Under the principle of relative values, all other things will thereupon become secondary. This process psychologists call sublimation.

Is this a counsel of acquiescence? Not at all. Those who are forty or fifty years old will recall the fable of the Wind and the Sun in one of the McGuffey readers. It seemed that they argued about which could first cause a certain traveler to remove his cloak. The Wind blew furiously, but the traveler clutched the garment more tightly about him; whereas he quickly discarded it when the quiet rays of the Sun fell upon him. After all, this is the message of the life of the chief character in "Goodbye, Mr. Chips." By inclination most teachers are not reformers. They are strongest when they let the silent influence of their lives play upon those they come in daily contact with, provided, of course, that their lives are normal, happy, cultivated ones. But they radiate no such influence when they develop compensatory complexes as disappointment or disillusionment comes their way.[2]

12. *The teacher should assume a citizen's rightful responsibility in the life of the community that the school serves.*

Perhaps happiest are those teachers who have made a place for themselves in the life of the community as well as in the life of the school, identifying themselves with social and civic groups and contributing to community life as do normal citizens in other walks of life. Certainly this is what the citizenry would expect of teachers. Perhaps only when teachers tend to withhold themselves from the

---

[2] Harlan C. Koch, "The Public as a Factor in the Mental Hygiene of Teachers," *School of Education Bulletin*, University of Michigan, March, 1940, pp. 97-98.

normal endeavors of the community are they considered different.

Recently in our city, the Public Schools and the Chamber of Commerce arranged a Business-Education Day, at which time all teachers were guests of business houses and industries. The teachers selected the types of business they wished to visit. The firms, in turn, used their top executives as hosts and arranged a full day's program, including tours, luncheons, and conferences. At the end of the day there was a general reaction that the affair should be repeated annually. In turn, there is to be arranged an Education-Business Day, when the business leaders will be scheduled to visit the schools. All schools will be hosts, and after the visits to classrooms there will be round table discussions treating the modern ways of education, just as there were tours and discussions on Business-Education Day treating the modern ways of business.

13. *The teacher at all times should reveal a love of our country and a leadership in establishing the American ideals ever firmer with the student.*

There was once a time when educators left citizenship teaching to the social studies program and, consequently, to those handling that program. More and more America is appreciating the true breadth of citizenship, and all teachers are being given credit for their share in undertaking the training. Those who pay taxes for schools take it for granted that the teachers in those schools are fully aware of the ideals of American life and are devoted to them. The teachers' love of country is to be demonstrated through their attitudes and energies in working with their pupils, as well as in their contributions to the American ideals through their out-of-school associations and endeavor. The person who does not feel these loyalties to the American heritage has no place in our classrooms.

The Strength of Teachers

14. *The one who enters teaching has no reason to apologize by either word or action for having done so.*

Nothing cheapens teaching more than for one who teaches to make apologies for the occupation to friends or associates. There are a number of people who still seem to be surprised that one with other talents has gone into teaching. The author has always been interested in art and at times has expressed himself in one art form or another. On more than one occasion, the display of some of his drawings has brought forth this remark, "Why did you ever go into teaching? You could have been an artist."

Yes, we in teaching might have been an artist, a salesman, a farmer, a statesman, an attorney, a housewife, a musician, or something equally as popular and important in the world of work. But we chose teaching, a field of work highly important in its own right—and a field that can bring a true feeling of that importance to the one doing the teaching if he will only accept the award.

We have all seen a few teachers whose indifference to the heavy responsibilities of the job cheapened the profession. We have all had a teacher somewhere along the line who by word or action apologized for being in the work or otherwise belittled the calling. One who casts reflections upon the occupation of his choice no doubt casts a few reflections upon himself.

15. *The teacher should take as much professional pride in his skill as the physician takes in his.*

For one who is studying to become a teacher, there is nothing as helpful and encouraging as to observe an efficient master teacher who is highly engrossed in his work, whose energy and finesse reveal true enjoyment and satisfaction. The thrill that comes to a student of teaching who observes such skillful manipulation of a classroom must be as great as that which comes to the medical interne who watches a master surgeon perform a skillful operation. The social significance of the one performance parallels that of the other.

For one who is studying to become a teacher, there is nothing as discouraging as to observe an experienced teacher whose manner and action reveal the absence of any spark of interest in the thing that he is doing. Pride in the profession grows with skill in teaching performance and wanes with the absence of it.

16. *Teaching is no stronger than its teachers.*

Teachers show their strength in two ways, through the actual instructional contribution in dealing with children and through their professional relationships with their teaching associates and the laymen. They reveal their weakness, and consequently the weakness of the profession, through these same two avenues.

Occasionally we find a teacher who is at home with the children and does a good job in the classroom, but who is eternally clashing with other teachers over school affairs and who has no time for the parent with a grievance. For instance, there was my teaching associate whose contribution in the classroom and the children's fine acceptance of him there were never appreciated by the faculty, for they got to know him as an obstructionist in faculty meeting discussions. There was a speech teacher whose commendable classroom work was tarnished each year by her clashes with pupils, other teachers, and parents, while coaching the senior play. And a kindergarten teacher who liked the children but was never understood by the parents. And a teacher who taught well but spent too much time in public criticizing the operation of the schools, from the actions of the board of education to the work of the teacher next door.

Teaching is no stronger than its teachers. And the real pillars of the profession are those who are consistently strong, outside as well as inside the classroom.

17. *The merits and accomplishments of the school should be common knowledge of the teacher who would promote the school's welfare with the public.*

Helping the public to understand the value of the work of the school demands of the teacher an appreciation of the school's merits and accomplishments. It is easier for a layman to make a disparaging remark about the school's work than it is for the teacher to have at hand a ready answer in the form of a true knowledge of the school's advantages and successes. In general, schools today, in both intensity and breadth, stand head and shoulders above those of the first quarter of this century. Consequently, in any school situation it behooves the teacher to ferret out the strengths of the program that have made this so.

Some of the advancements made this century in the elementary schools to be found in almost any section of the nation are these:

1. The improvement in reading instruction attested to by the ability of the average primary child to read and to understand the printed page. This reflects the research that has been carried out in this area and put to use all over the country. The hit-and-miss reading instruction of earlier days has been driven from most of our schools.

2. The close personal attention given to the individual pupil. This is reflected in the instructional management of the classroom by small segments, the correlation of testing and instruction, the congenial classroom atmosphere, the smaller classes, the special classes for the physically and the mentally handicapped, and the enrichment and breadth of the classroom program.

3. The self-confidence and facility of expression that are demonstrated by the average school child. This reflects the concerted effort made during the past quarter of a century to make a place in the classroom group for all the children there, not just the more alert. It reflects the emphasis placed upon oral expression, the concerted effort to help each child to get up on his feet and express his ideas before his classmates.

4. The extension of the elementary program to include such regular studies as instrumental music and science. This breadth has not sacrificed the basic instruction in reading, arithmetic, writing, and language. Improved techniques in teaching in the latter areas have accounted for this.

18. *The teacher who would defend his practices needs to appreciate fully why such practices are educationally more sound than others.*

The advancement that has been made in the use of manipulative devices in teaching number work has not come by chance. It has come through experimentation, based on the careful study of results of various instructional approaches. Behind the whole movement to team up manipulative devices with the pencil-and-paper work are basic principles of teaching.

The simplest formula for determining instructional practices is to determine first the goals of the program and then to select the practices most adequate to achieve those goals. To attack or to defend classroom practices in the abstract is illogical. The good teacher sees all of his planning and his procedures in relation to his goals of instruction and in relation to the pupils at hand.

Home study is an instructional practice of long standing. To argue about home study as a practice in the abstract, with no consideration of the goals of the program or the pupils being served is somewhat illogical.

WORKING WITH ASSOCIATES

19. *Good working conditions in a school are dependent upon pleasant relationships among the staff.*

A good school is something more than the total instructional output of the teachers, just as a good symphony orchestra is something more than the total output of its members. There is a harmonious atmosphere in a good school that seems to say that there exists a pleasant working relationship among the staff.

This harmony is not achieved by such a simple gesture as a pleasant good morning exchanged by the teachers as they pass on their way to the classrooms. It comes from a group appreciation of the importance of the joint undertaking and mutual respect of the opinions and energies of each staff member engaged in the work of the school. It is a wholesome atmosphere that assures pleasant relationships.

20. *The teacher's relationships with the other staff members should reveal a pleasant and cooperative spirit.*

Wholesome working conditions in a school, which keep morale at the high level necessary to good schools, are dependent upon each teacher rather than upon just a majority of teachers. We have all known the fine teachers who as they entered the school each day were able to leave their out-of-school troubles at the door. We have all known the few maladjusted teachers who were unable to do this and who consequently solicited the support of fellow worker or even pupil in carrying their burdens. We have all known the busy-body who spent her spare time passing on the gossip of the school system rather than at something that would mean a better education of the child.

The day-by-day relationships of teachers are most pleasant and co-operative when they have their setting in the welfare of the children. The beginning teacher who sizes up the faculty and is tempted to wonder what she'll ever have in common with Miss X is most apt to find that common denominator of human relationships in the education of a group of children. The best in teachers is revealed when they are co-operating to make the school's instructional contribution the best possible.

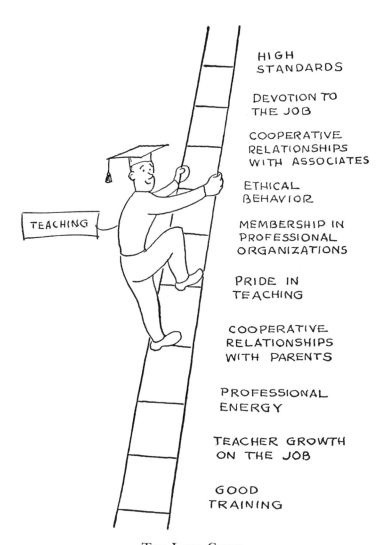

HIGH
STANDARDS

DEVOTION TO
THE JOB

COOPERATIVE
RELATIONSHIPS
WITH ASSOCIATES

ETHICAL
BEHAVIOR

MEMBERSHIP IN
PROFESSIONAL
ORGANIZATIONS

PRIDE IN
TEACHING

COOPERATIVE
RELATIONSHIPS
WITH PARENTS

PROFESSIONAL
ENERGY

TEACHER GROWTH
ON THE JOB

GOOD
TRAINING

TEACHING

THE LONG CLIMB

21. *In determining a balanced contribution to the extra-class duties to be handled in the school, a teacher follows his best professional judgment rather than the practices of another teacher.*

In any school there are a hundred and one duties to be performed outside the classroom. In group control, teacher service is called for in such places as the playground, the study hall, the cafeteria, the hallway, and the auditorium. At the secondary-school level can be added the many services connected with athletic contests, dramatic productions, school dances, and similar functions calling for the sale and the handling of tickets.

Another area of extra-class duty is that of activities calling for sponsorship—activities in which teachers give direct supervision to the pupils who engage in these activities. The list is just as broad as the ingenuity of teachers and pupils who plan this extra-curricular program. The more common fields of endeavor include inter-school athletics, dramatics, clubs, student government, publications, and intra-mural sports. The educational possibilities for pupils are far reaching and the instructional satisfactions for teachers are just as abundant.

Besides these more apparent services that lend themselves to assignment and schedule, in any school there are the miscellaneous week-by-week or day-by-day duties that somebody must carry out, the duties that seem to invite a willing worker. One week there are some standardized tests to be scored, and another an evening or two of decorating for a school festival. Perhaps an Open House is coming up and the program is dependent upon a teacher's volunteering to present some of the classroom work. There are always hallways and school bulletin boards inviting the careful attention of interested teachers. In almost any school a few children need after-school help on some evening, providing there are teachers willing to serve with pleasant spirit.

School administration in general can be expected to do the best job possible to distribute evenly the extra duties in the school. Needless to say, the variability among duties and among personnel make this impossible. However, there is little reason for a beginning teacher to approach the job with fear of inequality in his assignments. Better that he fear that he will not be given the opportunity to participate fully in the activities of the school, for only in doing so can he expect to secure the personal satisfaction that teachers deserve. If an experienced teacher is inclined to look askance at the eagerness and energy of the newcomer, the latter should not permit such apathy to dampen his enthusiasm.

22. *Any random comments about a child passed from one teacher to another should first stand the test of benefit to the child.*

In and about the school the members of a teaching staff have as common topics of conversation their work, their working conditions, and their pupils. These common interests are to be found in every school in the country. In such relationships ethical procedures suggest themselves as the commonsense approach to the job.

Some years ago the author in directing student teaching on a college campus had the opportunity to secure firsthand the reactions of the seniors to their first classroom experience, that of student teaching. Out of a class of over a hundred student teachers there was a significant number who came back to the campus shocked at what they recognized as unprofessional gossiping about pupils among the experienced teachers. Disparaging remarks passed in the faculty lunch and rest rooms took a bit of the professional enthusiasm from the beginners.

It is indeed unfortunate if a pupil's poor start in a school and the troubles in his life that he brings in from the outside are permitted to plague him throughout school because of the idle discussion of teachers. Such cases of treatment represent a minority, for the great majority of teachers certainly recognize and practice the truth of the statement made previously in this book, that teachers are in school to help rather than to judge children, to help them to walk better rather than to trip them in their uneven steps. When teachers talk across the lunch table about their pupils, such remarks should pass the test of promising benefit to the ones under discussion.

23. *The attack that a teacher makes upon the results of teaching at another level is in reality an attack upon his own position in the profession.*

As developed elsewhere in this book, a high school teacher may undermine the work of others in her profession by making slighting remarks about the instruction in the elementary school. A college professor or even a university president may speak out in public his misgivings about the preparation for college that high schools are giving their students. An elementary teacher may openly criticize the formality of the instruction in the local junior high school.

Just as often as these things happen, just that often the teaching profession is attacked from within. This is not to insinuate that our schools do not call for improvement at all levels. It is merely to say that such improvement calls for a considerate and cooperative attack upon the task. The open attack upon a fellow worker at another level, or upon his methods, is a poor substitute.

WORKING WITH ADMINISTRATORS

24. *A school administrator bears a double responsibility—to pupil and to teacher.*

Recently a young teacher complained to our office that she felt she was being supervised too closely by the principal. By "too closely" she referred to the principal's concern about lesson plans, the teacher's practices in grouping, the arrangement of the room for work, and the selection of materials. In additon to classroom observation, the supervison was including frequent after-school meetings of teacher groups.

It is difficult to say when a teacher is supervised too closely and when a teacher is not supervised enough. However, in this case it was apparent that the supervision "was not taking." Fine schools are dependent upon the continuous leadership that is afforded teachers through the efforts of administrators and supervisors. Any beginning teacher should expect and even demand his share of this attention.

The principal carries a heavy responsibility for the instruction and development of children and should certainly spend ample time at the job of securing proper learning conditions in the classrooms and the school as a whole. The wise administrator doesn't try to do this alone, but capitalizes upon the good work already being done by teachers in the school and the vicinity.

If at times supervision seems oppressive to the teacher it may reflect the over-anxiety of the supervisor to carry out this responsibility to instruction, or it may mean that supervision has become a fetish. These faults will be avoided if the supervisor appreciates fully the second responsibility, the responsibility to the teacher.

Supervision may seem oppressive when there exists a state of poor conditions in the classroom. Any help that is to come to a teacher through supervision is dependent upon mutual respect of the two parties. Each must fully respect the position of the other, the teacher seeing the supervisor's responsibility and the supervisor realizing the teacher's significant position with the class. The teacher must be receptive to help, without being utterly dependent upon it. In turn, the supervisor must be respectful of the teacher's significance in the classroom and do everything possible to build it up and nothing to tear it down.

25. Supervision can be friendly and helpful at the same time that it is businesslike and realistic.

The pleasant relationship that is invited between supervisor and teacher by no means outlaws a businesslike approach in supervision. In classroom supervision, time of both parties will be wasted unless they consider realistically the teaching and learning going on and the question of how it might be improved.

The teacher being supervised can enter the spirit of the thing much better if she, too, places her mind upon the improvement of instruction. For either party to look upon supervision as a personal matter will defeat the purpose. Recently a young teacher left the employ of our schools after coming to the conclusion that he would not be able to bring the learning conditions of his classroom up to the level that the children deserved. This conclusion came after the principal and supervisors had given the classroom a lot of supervisory attention. It was remarkable how well the teacher had fallen into the spirit of the supervisory effort, sensing quite clearly the classroom conditions that were being sought, the conditions that the children deserved. In the end, he realized that he could not provide those conditions as a teacher. For one teacher who cannot profit by supervision, there are a dozen others who move ahead through it to better practices.

26. *For a teacher to hide instructional difficulties is to be unfair to both himself and his pupils.*

Supervision has two features, that of helping teachers improve their programs and that of judging the effectiveness of teachers' work. The latter duty cannot be escaped by school administration.

However, some teachers, in magnifying this latter feature of supervision out of proper relationship to the former, build up a fear of supervision. They wish to hide their classroom difficulties from the administration. Such action is quite shortsighted. It denies the basic purpose of supervision and, furthermore, invites the multiplication of difficulties to the point at which it will be too late for supervision to help. The beginning teacher who finds it easy to confide in the administrator is indeed fortunate.

27. *The teacher shall not limit his activities to the classroom but shall participate actively in the extra-curricular life of the school.*

As indicated more than once in this book, the work in the classroom is but a portion of the teaching that goes on around a school. The teacher should participate actively in the total program of the school. School teaching includes the entire job.

28. *The teacher must meet time schedules promptly, keep registers and other records accurately, and file promptly the reports called for in the management of the school.*

This principle of teaching speaks for itself. The routine management of the classroom and the school system calls for these extras from the teacher. They cannot be neglected.

29. *The higher the level of working conditions in a school, the greater responsibility of both teacher and administrator to the investing public.*

School administration works hard to improve the working conditions in a school system. Teachers, in turn, help to effect those conditions through the quality of their teaching contributions and through ethical procedures in working for teacher welfare. Parent groups catch the spirit and serve to pass bond issues and to increase budgets. As the working conditions for teachers in a school system keep improving, it behooves teachers to work all the harder to do a good job of instruction.

In review—the young teacher who enters the classroom to teach second grade, American history, algebra, or whatnot soon realizes that he is teaching among a mass of interested, or at least curious, people. In addition to the children, there are the parents, the citizens who meet him on out-of-school occasions, the other teachers, the principal, the superintendent, and all the special staff who have a direct or remote connection with his classroom. In a sense he works in a glass case, for his actions are under close observation. In another sense, it isn't a glass case, for his classroom reaches out to tie into the hustle and bustle of the community life. That's where his work finds its true meaning.

Topics for Study and Discussion

1. Accepting the proposal that teaching is a matter of human relationships, that a teacher is always dealing with people, list the personal characteristics that this seems to demand of a person entering teaching.

2. Explain the unique position that a teacher holds in the school's public relations program.

3. Bring before the group an officer of an active Parent-Teacher Association who can explain the program of the organization.

4. Have school communities in the past made any unreasonable demands of teachers relative to their personal or civic life?

5. To what extent do you feel that Dr. Koch expresses the sentiment of teachers in general?

6. What do expenditures for schools in this geographical area indicate about public attitude toward schools?

7. List a half dozen major suggestions for a teacher's code of professional ethics.

8. List a half dozen suggestions for a group of teachers wishing to advance the level of the profession.

Chapter 14

The Teacher's Welfare

THE HIGHWAY OF AMERICAN EDUCATION LEADING FROM THE past is studded with the Horace Manns who waged the fight to elevate teaching to its present professional status. Much of this struggle was centered around the need of an adequate program of professional training and adequate certification requirements. Early school leaders realized that the cheaper the training, the cheaper the calling would remain.

One of the staunch band of educators who tenaciously attacked the notion that anybody who showed an inclination to "keep school" could teach was John Swett, the West Coast's contribution to that early struggle. Writing on the subject in 1884, Swett pointed out that out of the 300,000 teachers in the United States at that time only one in ten was a graduate of a normal school.[1] Today, with over three times that many teachers, the profession can boast that the ratio of training-institution graduates has been reversed. Furthermore, the initial course is much longer, and graduate study beyond that course is the common practice.

---

1 John Swett, *Methods of Teaching*, New York: Harper & Brothers, 1884.

As the profession has increased its contribution to the supporting public in the way of better teachers and consequently better classrooms, so in return the public has provided the profession with better working conditions. Although there is no nationwide uniformity in these conditions, the welfare of teachers today is characterized by tenure measures, health benefits, salary schedules, retirement laws, provisions for leaves of absence, and similar benefits that mark the public-school teacher as a person of legal status and the calling as one offering security in exchange for an efficient contribution.

Furthermore, the beginning teacher may count among his blessings the opportunity to advance in the profession to better positions. If he will only take advantage of them, available to him in this advancement in both welfare status and teaching position are the services of professional associations, such as the National Education Association and such kindred agencies as the United States Office of Education. This chapter represents an attempt to do no more than introduce to the beginning teacher some of the more common welfare provisions and the work of the National Education Association and the United States Office of Education.

The Welfare of the Child

1. *The welfare of the teacher is so interlocked with the welfare of the child that it is impossible to secure the one without the other.*

Much is written and said about the welfare of the teacher; and very often it is implied that teacher welfare is something that can be extracted from the teaching situation and placed on a table for consideration alone. It can't. Teacher welfare is so intertwined with pupil welfare that its discussion demands full respect for the bonds that tie the two together.

As was indicated in Chapter 13, the teaching profession advances only as the instruction of children and youth advances. If the classrooms are doing a poor job in the

FOLLOW ME

PUPIL WELFARE   TEACHER WELFARE

management and instruction of pupils, the welfare of the teachers will likewise suffer. School patrons are reluctant to vote more money for salaries and to endorse increased welfare measures if they have a poor feeling about the work of the schools. In fact, if classroom results are poor the public is likely to question such existing benefits as tenure and extended vacations. On the other hand, when there is a good public reaction to the work of the schools, when the welfare of the pupils is well cared for, then may teachers expect public support of steps to improve teacher welfare.

In our profession there have grown up two types of teachers' organizations. The first of these is the association that has as its goal the improvement of instruction or administration at a particular level. For instance, an English teacher may join the National Council of the Teachers of English and through it receive help in improving her instructional program. It might be said that all of this type of teachers' associations have their origin in the welfare of the child. They have as their goal the improvement of the conditions of instruction.

The other type of organization is the one set up to serve teacher welfare. These associations or federations seldom give time to problems of instruction but limit the energies of their members to matters pertaining to improving the working conditions of teachers. Typical activities might include the advancement of a new salary schedule, an improved schedule of health-leave benefits, and state legislation pertaining to teacher tenure. Although teacher welfare is the goal here, it can be reasoned that good working conditions for teachers promise good learning conditions for children.

Needless to say, both the welfare of the child and that of the teacher are essential to a good school situation. Small classes, fine classrooms, abundant supplies and equipment, and an excellent curriculum will not result in a good school unless teachers are adequately paid and otherwise respected. On the other hand, the value of measures advancing the teacher's status can be measured by checking their implications for pupil welfare. For instance, if a tenure law is so constructed that it eliminates a probationary period of trial in teaching, then its possible harm to children marks it as harmful to the profession. If a proposed salary schedule must be financed by robbing the budget accounts for needed textbooks and supplies, then its harm to children marks it as harmful to teachers as well. And so—

2. *Regardless of the purposes for which it is formed, any teachers' organization that has the good of the profession at heart will devote a fair proportion of its energies to the welfare of the pupils.*

3. *There is no more promising way to secure better working conditions of a lasting nature for teachers than to effect better learning conditions for pupils.*

4. *Teacher growth on the job is as essential to a good school program as proper preparation for it.*

It is one thing to secure the preparation necessary to secure certification for teaching and acceptance for the first position; it is another to continue one's preparation while teaching. Commonly accepted today among teachers and administrators is the conviction that training of an organized nature does not stop when teaching begins. Although colleges carry the major share of the responsibility for this advanced training, there is an increasing tendency for school systems to accept a responsibility in the matter. Such activities are commonly spoken of as *in-service training.*

In-service training in a local school system is an extension of the idea of good supervision. Years ago, the latter was limited to the supervision of the teacher's work in the classroom and was an individualized process involving only the teacher and the supervisor. In time the scope of supervision broadened to include the improvement of teaching through group activities involving a number of teachers. Committee work, professional faculty meetings,

GROWTH ON THE JOB IS AN ESSENTIAL TO TEACHING

conferences led by visiting instructional leaders, and similar group efforts emerged as accepted supervisory practices.

In recent years have been added salary schedules providing automatic salary increments from year to year and often including the stipulation that the teacher in return secure two or three additional courses every three or four years. These two practices, broadened programs of supervision and increment salary schedules, have resulted in the provision of in-service training by the local school administration. It represents a standardization of some of the group activities of the program of supervision, and where needed, such effort meets salary increment provisions. Among such in-service courses that bring returns to the local school system have been: the development of a new home report card, a survey of science instruction in the local schools and the development of teaching guides, the development of a series of film strips for the third-grade study of the local community, and the development of a booklet to go to the homes of the children entering the kindergarten or first grade.

A teacher's development on the job is not limited to the organization of group study programs such as those just described. The wise teacher is one who sizes up his own needs and plans a program to meet them. If there are no local in-service programs and if there is no graduate school close by—as is the case with such a large percentage of America's teachers—teacher ingenuity still sees to it that development takes place.

TEACHER TENURE

5. *Good teachers deserve security in their positions.*

Many states by law afford the teacher protection against local dismissal without good cause. Fifteen states afford this protective tenure on a statewide basis. Fifteen others grant tenure protection in only part of the state. In the case of the latter, tenure is usually compulsory for the larger school districts and in the smaller either doesn't apply or is made optional.

A tenure law provides that after a probationary period, usually two to four years, a teacher cannot be dismissed without good cause and formal procedure. The causes of dismissal, such as inefficiency in teaching or immoral conduct, are prescribed by law. The formal procedure includes written notice before a certain date in the school year, a statement of the reasons, and an opportunity for self-defense. The latter may provide a hearing before the Board of Education or an appeal for court hearing.

In the case of the probationary period, which is a period of trial employment, the Board of Education may give notice in writing to the teacher before a certain date that his services will be terminated at the end of the school year, at the end of the period for which he has been employed.

Tenure laws have worked both to the advantage and to the disadvantage of teachers. In many rural areas and small school districts in the states governed by such laws, it has been customary for the school trustees to fear the principle of tenure and consequently to dismiss their teachers just prior to qualifying for tenure. For this reason the teachers in such areas saw little if any protection or security in such laws. Consequently, in many states the law governs only the larger school systems.

6. *The weak and ineffective teacher is the greatest threat to the security that good teachers deserve.*

The school patron wants good schools and naturally is not in sympathy with school laws that protect inefficient and weak teachers. The protection to teachers that comes with the passage of a tenure act implies that this security for teachers will be balanced by a high standard of teaching performance.

Teachers need to realize that the weak teacher represents a threat to their security. For the greater the percentage of inadequately handled classrooms, the greater the patrons' doubt about the advisability of tenure laws. Good tenure laws imply good working conditions under which teachers can keep their minds on their work rather than upon their personal security. They also imply the profession's recognition that poor teaching performance cannot be tolerated.

7. *Provision for sick leave is increasing as a practice in the advancement of teacher welfare.*

Perhaps about ninety-nine per cent of the beginning teachers in accepting their first position limit their consideration of its financial benefits to the salary alone. Little if any thought is given to the absence or presence of other dollars-and-cents values of the position, such as retirement provisions, disability benefits, or sick leave allowances. But strangely enough, the variation in such practices among states and among school systems presents a financial variable often greater than the salary variable. Some of the facts about sick leave are these: [2]

> By state law, seven states assure the teacher ten days of sick leave with pay annually. Ten others allow a smaller number.
>
> Most of these seventeen states permit the accumulation of such sick leave to a limited degree. For instance, sick leave in California is accumulative to 40 days, in Iowa to 35, in Tennessee to 36, and in Wisconsin to 30.

---

[2] National Education Association, "Teachers in the Public Schools," *Research Bulletin*, Vol. 27, No. 4, 1949.

By far, most of the states make no such demands upon their local school systems, and consequently the granting of sick leave with pay is left to the discretion of the local board of education.

In the case of states with teacher retirement laws, it is customary to provide disability allowance to a teacher who becomes permanently disabled prior to normal retirement. Ten years of service is the typical number of years one must serve before qualifying for such disability allowance. However, the range by states is from five to twenty-five years of service.

Although the states that assure teachers protection against temporary sickness and disability are few, there is a noticeable tendency in the direction of this type of welfare among states and among local school systems.

8. *There is no substitute for membership in a good professional association of teachers.*

Every state in the Union has its state association of teachers. In as many as a third of the states the membership is one hundred per cent of the total number of instructional employees, and in no state does the membership fall below 74 per cent. There are thousands of local associations of teachers that are likewise active in the study of the profession.

Almost half a million teachers and school administrators belong to the National Education Association, which is somewhere between 40 and 50 per cent of the teachers of the country. There are national associations organized to serve every subject field. The English teacher, the science teacher, the primary teacher, the elementary principal, and any other teacher can find an organization that serves his particular field of work. The thousands of journals, bulletins, and yearbooks issued each year by these groups help to attest to the great professional contribution that they make. There is no substitute for membership in a good professional association.

THE NATIONAL EDUCATION ASSOCIATION

The National Education Association of the United States, which supports and is supported by almost a half million memberships, is commonly spoken of as the NEA. As stated in its charter the organization's goals are quite clear: *To elevate the character and advance the interests of the profession of teaching and to promote the course of popular education in the United States.*

A bulk of the members are classroom teachers, who feel the satisfaction of unification with a strong national movement to elevate teaching. The NEA carries on its work through a representative assembly, elected officers, appointed committees and commissions, a headquarters staff of 200 in Washington, D. C., 29 departments, 51 affiliated state and territorial associations, and nearly 2900 affiliated local and sectional associations. The twenty-nine groups recognized as departments are independent organizations in specialized fields, with elected officers and professional programs.

The representative assembly, of about 2800 representatives from the local affiliated groups, meets each July to conduct the business of the Association. It determines policies, approves the budget, hears the reports of committees, passes resolutions, and creates new departments and special study groups. The work and interests of the

Association are reflected in this list of goals adopted at one of the annual meetings of the Representative Assembly:

1. Active democratic local education associations in every community including a Future Teachers of America chapter in every college which prepares teachers, affiliated with the state and national associations.

2. A strong and effective state education association in every state.

3. A larger and more aggressive national education association.

4. Unified dues—local, state, and national—collected by the local.

5. A membership enrolment of at least 90 per cent in local, state, and national professional organizations.

6. Unified committees—the chairmen of local and state committees serving as advisory members of corresponding national committees.

7. A professionally prepared and competent teacher in every classroom.

8. A professionally prepared and competent principal at the head of every school.

9. A professionally prepared and competent administrator at the head of each school system.

10. A strong, adequately-staffed state department of education in each state and a more adequate Federal education agency.

11. A professional salary for all members of the profession, adjusted to the increased cost of living.

12. Professional security for teachers and administrators guaranteed by effective tenure legislation.

13. Retirement income for old age and disability.

14. Cumulative sabbatical and sick leave.

15. Reasonable class size and equitable distribution of the teaching load.

16. Informed lay support of public education at local, state, and national levels.

17. Units of school administration large enough to provide for efficient operation, with special attention to the needs of rural areas and stronger state and local boards of education.

18. Adequate educational opportunity for every child regardless of race, creed, color, or residence.

19. The equalization and expansion of educational opportunity including needed state and national financing.

20. A safe, healthful, and wholesome community environment for every child.

21. An effective and adequately financed United Nations Educational, Scientific, and Cultural Organization.

THE UNITED STATES OFFICE OF EDUCATION

Acting as one of the two chief fountainheads of national attention to school affairs is the United States Office of Education. Established by an Act of Congress in 1867, it has continued through the years to promote the cause of better schools throughout the nation. Capitalizing upon the common problems faced by schools, it collects and analyzes pertinent statistics, gives advice and leadership in all areas of administration and instruction, advances international educational relations, promotes improvements in the profession, and administers a number of educational grants. In all of its efforts, the Office of Education respects the fact that the responsibility for education is vested in the respective states.

The efforts of the office staff of 200 professional people

are concentrated through six divisions, each of which bears relationship to some broad field of school operation. The brief resume of the work of these departments that follows is not adequate to express the full import of the Office of Education.

The Division of Elementary and Secondary Schools deals with problems of school organization, instructional problems, and education of exceptional children. On its staff are specialists for various age groups, for different subjects, and for special areas such as testing and adult education. The division is particularly concerned with the teaching of health, science, social sciences, fine and industrial arts.

The Higher Education Division is subdivided into three units dealing with organization, professional education, and arts and sciences. In the organization unit are experts in Negro education, junior colleges, land-grant colleges, and business management. The professional education department is concerned primarily with the fields of health, engineering, and teacher training; the arts and sciences unit with the social and physical sciences.

The Vocational Education Division is charged with administering the national Vocational Education Acts, which provide grants-in-aid to the States. These grants cover five areas of occupational education: agriculture, business, home economics, trade and industrial, and occupational information and guidance. Between 25 and 30 million dollars are appropriated each year for vocational education. In addition to allocating these Federal funds which are always matched by state funds, the division works with state boards in planning their programmes.

Within *the Division of School Administration* the focus is primarily on making Federal services available through state departments of education to local school administrators. The Division works closely with the National Council of Chief State School Officers. It assists local administrators in solving problems of school housing, pupil transportation, school finances and business management, and school health services. The disposal of surplus Federal property and legislation affecting schools are also major concerns of this division.

The Division of International Educational Relations promotes international understanding by operating exchange programs for teachers and students, publishing studies on foreign educational systems, preparing materials on international educational relations, and evaluating foreign credentials. It is organized into three geographic units—American Republics, European education, Near and Far Eastern education.

The work of *the Division of Central and Auxiliary Services* cuts across the jurisdictions of the other divisions. Its services include a research and statistical service, an information and publications service, and a service to libraries. It also has two services dealing with the educational uses of radio and visual aids. The budget and fiscal service and the personal service are found in this division.

The Office publishes two periodicals, *School Life,* issued monthly and addressed primarily to administrators and teachers of elementary and secondary schools, and *Higher Education,* issued semi-monthly and addressed to college and university administrators and faculty. In addition, each year scores of pamphlets and studies of a special nature are issued and distributed widely. The Office is at the service of any individual teacher just as much as it is to any school system.

ADVANCEMENT IN TEACHING

Movement among teachers in the profession is the normal thing. While one remains for years in the same position for which she is first hired, another moves from school to school, from state to state, or from classroom to administrative post. Regardless of his future, the beginning teacher has little time to think about the next job. His immediate challenge is the classroom at hand, and his firm establishment there is the best preparation for the eventualities of the career ahead.

9. *As an initial step to advancement an impression of merit on one's associates is generally as significant as an impression on one's superior officers.*

It does not take a group of teachers long to determine the contributions that each is making to the total school situation and the contribution that each is capable of making. The process of appraisal of effort and ability that goes on among teachers in any school faculty or school system brings to light the teachers who know how to get things done. As instructional jobs come and go, it is not by chance that the same people keep bobbing up as committee chairmen. Their election to the posts represents the faith of their fellow teachers in their leadership qualities.

In any school system there exists this established leadership of certain teachers, and seldom is it overlooked as appointments come along for department headships, assistant principalships, and other administrative and supervisory positions. The author once knew a teacher in a large school who was so busy trying to make an impression on his principal that he never found time to do his own work nor did his fellow teachers ever give him a second thought in their selection of chairmen and spokesmen.

Most school systems fill their supervisory and administrative positions by promoting within the ranks. In making recommendations for such appointments, seldom does the superintendent make a mistake by trying to determine the teachers who have already established themselves as leaders with their fellow teachers, their principals, and their supervisors. Leadership among one's immediate associates promises success in positions calling for leadership over larger groups of teachers.

Professional Energy. A leader of teachers who revealed repeated interest in the bases for professional promotion was Dewitt S. Morgan, who died a few years ago in the service of the Indianapolis schools as superintendent. In summarizing the distinctive qualities that cause a teacher's merit to be recognized by professional associates, he made this statement in behalf of professional energy:

> One quality which stands out might well be called *professional energy.* It is a quality which certain ones possess and which brings definite accomplishment. In one case it produces professional studies in written form; in another, it develops new forms of student activities in a school; in another, it inaugurates an improved program of school-community relations; in another, it develops new materials for a course of study; in another, it inaugurates a program of professional study among associates.
>
> Wherever professional energy abounds, something happens. If it really lives, it cannot be suppressed by any short-sighted official discouragement, nor can it ever be thwarted by limited material facilities. True

professional energy will break through these oft-mentioned barriers and somehow, in some way, produce very distinctive results. Whenever it does, it will be recognized by associates, and superior officers cannot help but find it out. The really sound basis for professional promotion is concrete evidence of some form of professional achievement resulting from abounding professional energy. This is a general principle which applies in any case involving professional promotion.[3]

10. *Success in one's present position is the prerequisite to consideration for promotion.*

Most beginning teachers place their minds completely on the job at hand; this they should do. A few start their career thinking of a higher position, possibly some administrative post, and consequently look to their classroom as a mere stepping stone to something ahead.

Although there are always exceptions to the rule, in general those who move to better positions in teaching do so on the success that was demonstrated in the positions from which they moved. No teacher is going to demonstrate such success if his interest and attention are diverted to the post ahead. A good rule for a person to follow in accepting appointment is to be sure that each position accepted is one in which he can be happy and one in which he can make a success. To accept a position merely as a possible steppingstone to another is indeed a professional gamble that may result in an unhappy career. Getting ahead means nothing in itself. What counts in the long run is getting ahead into work for which a person shows ability and promise. There is no reason that one

[3] Dewitt S. Morgan, "Bases for Professional Promotion," *The Phi Delta Kappan*, Vol. 24, No. 9, May, 1942, pp. 343-344.

EFFICIENT AND HIGHLY
PROFESSIONAL TEACHERS

INEFFECTIVE AND
UNETHICAL TEACHER

THOSE WHO DESERVE PROTECTION

should not by additional training and experience prepare himself for the possibility of advancement, but in doing so he should not neglect improvement of his performance in the position that he holds.

11. *In moving ahead in the profession advanced degrees are no substitute for experience.*

Recently a young man came to our office to apply for an administrative position in the local schools. Although he had taught only two years he pointed out that he felt he could not accept a classroom teaching position but must seek a principalship. He had just completed his doctorate in the school of education of a good West Coast university. He felt that because of his great investment in time and money in administrative training he could not afford to return to a classroom but must secure an administrative position.

What he had failed to see was that the people of our city had also made a great investment in schooling and that in being true to that investment our office could not afford to consider for an administrative post a candidate with such limited experience. The young applicant was asking for a consideration that he conscientiously felt that he deserved. He rightfully placed pride in his achievement in training. In other words, in throwing himself into prolonged graduate study after only two years of teaching, he maneuvered himself into the peculiar position of not being true to himself if he returned to the classroom.

Most undergraduates preparing to teach take it for granted that they will accept a position upon completion of the work for the first college degree. However, a small percentage seem to face the alternative of remaining on campus to complete the master's degree before accepting a position. The decision calls for careful thought and a realistic study of employment practices in the geographical area in which employment is eventually to be sought. A point in favor of completing the second degree immediately is that today it is common practice for school systems to follow salary schedules that place a higher monetary value upon the master's degree than upon the bachelor's. School systems having such scales usually place a differential of two or three hundred dollars between the two. The schedule included in Chapter 10 recognizes this distinction.

As to the advantage of the extra college study in handling the classroom situation, at this initial stage of teaching it is doubtful if the extra year of courses means much more to the trainee than the original four years, since both the four-year course and the five-year course are devoid of actual teaching experience other than student teachings. The author has concluded that graduate study in education done in connection with teaching experience has far greater value than a similar amount of graduate study done prior to experience in the classroom. Perhaps an ideal way for a teacher to secure a master's degree is to devote to the task the necessary summers of study while holding a teaching position. The course work takes on added meaning due to the student's teaching, and enables him to integrate study and experience through the period. Advanced study certainly aids one in his experience, but it cannot be substituted for such experience.

PROVISIONS FOR TEACHER RETIREMENT

Teachers' state retirement laws that are in effect contain so many complicated provisions, involving qualifications for retirement and benefit allowances paid, that it is indeed difficult for a teacher of some experience to understand all the features of the law. The first thing about such a law that a beginner learns is the amount of his monthly contribution to the retirement fund, for this is deducted from his salary check without his being consulted. This induction into the system should be sufficiently impressive to arouse the teacher's curiosity about the benefits eventually available.

The basic principle of financing a retirement system is the matching of contributors' funds with public funds. New Mexico and Delaware have the only state systems in which there is an exception to this. A member's contributions usually represent a stated percentage of his salary, often 4 or 5 per cent. There are many variations of these two common principles of management. Recently the Research Office of the National Education Association summarized qualifications for retirement allowances with this statement:

> In twenty-two states teachers may retire upon reaching a designated age, usually sixty, without meeting any service requirements other than possibly in the computation of average final salary; in twenty-two states teachers may retire after a designated number of years of service, regardless of age; and in twenty-five states there are both age and service requirements. Obviously, many states have alternative provisions.[4]

In a few cities there are local retirement systems operating separate from and in addition to the state retirement

---

[4] National Education Association, "Teachers in the Public Schools," *Research Bulletin*, Vol. 27, No. 4, 1949, p. 151.

plans. In such instances a teacher makes contributions to both systems and receives benefits from both.

12. *A full appreciation of the job of teaching does not accompany the teacher to his first position, but is something that grows on a person as he continues in the profession.*

It is a little too much to expect of a beginner a clear insight into all the interlocking factors that make up the teaching position. It might be said that this is hardly necessary to the success of the beginner. Especially remote during the first year is the significance of welfare provisions.

The author will never forget the shock that came with the pay check at the end of the first month in his first teaching position—to find that some of the salary had been retained for the retirement fund in keeping with Indiana state regulations. Other beginners felt the same surprise, and they joked about the cut that had been made to provide wheel-chairs for the more aged teachers. The wheel-chair stage of life seemed far removed, and the need of the young teacher for ready cash was much more pressing and apparent than old-age security. It was natural for a beginner to question why he shouldn't have the right to determine membership in a pension system.

Although provisions for retirement are a little far removed from the thinking of most young teachers, it is inevitable that with a few years on the job there come the awareness of and a growing concern for such provisions. The author's experience is as good as another's to develop this point. After seventeen years of service in the Indiana schools, he changed to a school position in Illinois. He found that he could withdraw his payments from the Indiana retirement fund. He turned to the Illinois teachers' retirement board and asked to buy up back teaching experience in that system, equivalent to the seventeen years he had taught in Indiana. But that state limited the recognition of previous experience to ten years. Although as a beginner he had wondered why anyone should dare deduct from his salary for retirement, now his position was completely reversed as he thought it unfair that moving across a state line should deprive him of credit in a retirement system equivalent to seven years of his teaching service.

After serving three years in Illinois, he took a position in New Jersey and went there with a total of twenty years of teaching experience. Again, the New Jersey retirement board would recognize only ten years of previous teaching experience, half of his total. Three years later he took a position in California, and the climax came when that state recognized in its retirement system no previous teaching experience. As far as service credited toward retirement, with twenty-three years' experience behind him, his position in the California retirement system was equivalent to that of a beginner just off the campus.

This example from the area of teacher welfare is given not as something too meaningful to the beginner who reads this book, but rather as an example of one of the many factors of the teaching position that grow in significance with experience. One may advance in the profession but at the same time he may sacrifice such welfare benefits as tenure and retirement rights. Other examples could be taken from such areas as classroom procedures, public relationships, professional advancement, and professional ethics.

Hidden behind the example just described is the fact that public education in America is a state and not a Federal responsibility. If it is a concept that means little more to a beginner than a bare statement in an educational textbook, in time its significance will grow. If he crosses state lines in following his trade, the difficulties faced in securing recertification, in losing tenure status, and in readjusting retirement plans will bring the statement to life—to his own life.

Although most school administrators or writers would agree to the fact that the first-year teacher need not see the complete potentialities and ramifications of the teaching position, there is little agreement as to what he should appreciate about it that first year. This fact is attested to by the great variation in the contents of the books issued as an introduction to teaching. We trust that the contents of this book have helped a bit in bringing into clearer view the realities of teaching.

Conclusion

13. *Principles of teaching take on meaning to a teacher only as practice of them in the classroom is added to the study of them that was afforded on campus.*

Every teacher has his own set of principles, his own teaching kit. This book has discussed only a small portion of the practices of the profession. And in closing, we might list a few more principles that invite discussion:

14. Interest enhances effort.

15. Learning takes place better when the pupil knows

where he is going and when that place is somewhere that he wants to go.

16. Continued growth of the child is dependent upon continued growth of the teacher.

17. A teacher may tire a class, just as a class may tire the teacher.

18. The pupil stands as the center of the organization of the school, and the teacher sees that the thing goes around.

19. The right method for one classroom teacher may be the wrong one for another.

20. Lasting education is not a matter of teacher-telling, but rather one of pupil-doing.

21. Whenever the pressure of time in the classroom forces a choice between conformity and originality in the work that the pupil is doing, the teacher should cast her lot with the latter.

22. A teacher who uses undemocratic practices in the classroom can hardly expect to impress the student with a true appreciation of democracy.

23. It is as important for the teacher to know the child as it is to know the subject matter.

24. Modification of behavior in the learner is the most effective measure of an educational program.

25. A single standard of attainment for a class has nothing in common with an appreciation of individual differences.

Topics for Study and Discussion

1. From experience with school situations give examples of the close relationship of teacher welfare and pupil welfare.

2. With the type of salary schedule that provides automatic increments is implied teacher growth on the job. To what extent is it necessary for school administration to provide means of such development and to what extent should such growth be taken for granted?

3. To what extent is it desirable to maintain a salary policy that places a financial premium upon superior teaching?

4. Secure from the National Education Association literature explaining the workings and the services of this national teachers' organization.

5. Explain the major features of the teacher tenure laws of this state. Study the schools' experience with the tenure system to determine its possible strong and weak points.

6. Secure from the National Education Association this pamphlet reviewing teacher retirement practices and compare the local situation with other sections of the nation: Research Bulletin, Vol. 28, No. 4, December, 1950, *Public-School Retirement at the Half Century.*

7. To what extent has the state provided a retirement system that assures a teacher of long experience some promise of security in old age?

Index

A

Ability grouping, 99, 146, 148, 152, 257
Absence from school, 141-142
Academy, the, 73-74
Acceleration through the grades, 50-52
Activity approach to education, 54-55, 95-96, 161-163
Adams, John, 65
Administration:
duties of, 301-302
justification of, 256-257
Adulthood as the goal of schooling, 50-51, 108-111, 162
Advancement in the teaching profession, 324-327
Alabama, 139
Alcohol and narcotics, 181
American Council on Education, 227
American way of life, 9, 44-49, 138-139, 265, 290-291
Applications for positions, 229
Arizona, 139
Arkansas, 139
Assignments, 102-103, 117-118
Attacks upon schools from within, 291-292, 300-301
Authority in supervision, 268-269
Average daily attendance, 82

B

Beginning teacher, the:
control of pupils, 236-240
knowing the pupils, 241-243
opening the term, 243-245
securing a position, 206-233

Beginning teacher, the (cont'd):
suggestions for success, 234-236
supervision of, 245-251
Berkeley, Governor, 65

C

California, 36, 83, 111, 139, 141, 222, 315
Carnegie, unit-and-credit plan, 108-110
Certification of teachers, 31-32, 223
Chewning, John O., 118-119
Citizenship, education for, 44-47, 96-98, 130-131, 144, 179-181
Civic participation of teachers, 289-290
Club program, 175
Colleges, enrollment of, 33
Colorado, 139
Community, participation of teacher in life of, 135, 289-290
Compulsory schooling, 138-142
Conformity confused with learning, 103-104
Connecticut, 87, 139, 141
Contest between teacher and pupil, 123-124
Contractual status, 230-231
Control of pupils, 125-131, 145, 236-240
Cooperative endeavor, 48, 98-99, 241
Courses offered in teacher preparation, 4-7
Cumulative record, 151, 241
Curriculum, the:
change in, 173-178
goals of, 156-160
nature of, 160-163
pupil's relationship to, 163-169